Roberts Brothers

Holy songs, carols, and sacred ballads

Roberts Brothers

Holy songs, carols, and sacred ballads

ISBN/EAN: 9783742899972

Manufactured in Europe, USA, Canada, Australia, Japa

Cover: Foto ©Thomas Meinert / pixelio.de

Manufactured and distributed by brebook publishing software
(www.brebook.com)

Roberts Brothers

Holy songs, carols, and sacred ballads

Holy Songs,

Carols, and Sacred Ballads.

BOSTON:
ROBERTS BROTHERS.
1880.

UNIVERSITY PRESS:
JOHN WILSON & SON, CAMBRIDGE.

Contents.

	PAGE
" *For none of us liveth to himself, and no man dieth to himself* "	9
" *Though I take the wings of the morning* "	11
" *God is the Lord which has showed us light* "	13
" *I have loved thee with an everlasting love* "	14
" *And fell on his neck, and kissed him* "	16
" *Let us now go even unto Bethlehem* "	17
" *Blessed are ye that weep now* "	20
" *The Lord our God is one Lord* "	22
" *Behold the man* "	24
" *What aileth thee, Hagar?* "	26
" *Let my prayer come before Thee: incline Thine ear unto my cry* "	27
" *If any man will come to Me, and hate not . . . his own life also, he cannot be My disciple* "	29
" *I am poor and needy, yet the Lord heareth me* "	30
" *Behold, I stand at the door* "	32
" *And there were shepherds* "	34
" *Praise is comely* "	36
" *We bring you good tidings* "	40
" *The time of the singing of birds is come* "	42
" *Out of the deep, out of the deep* "	44
" *If we be dead with Him, we shall also live with Him* "	45
" *Come unto Me* "	47
" *And I said, Oh that I had wings like a dove* "	49
" *What I say unto you I say unto all, Watch* "	51

" *Consider the lilies of the field* " 54
" *In Him we live, and move, and have our being* ". . . . 56
" *As the hart panteth* " 57
" *Lord, what is man?* " 58
" *Ye also, as lively stones, are built up a spiritual house* " . 60
" *He made the stars also* " 62
" *He hath put the world in their hearts* " 63
" *Surely the bitterness of death is past* " 64
" *And He carried me away in the spirit to a great and high mountain, and showed me that great city, the holy Jerusalem* " 66
" *There was darkness* " 68
" *It was the eve of the Sabbath* " 71
" *They went and made the sepulchre sure, sealing the stone and setting a watch* " 73
" *While it was yet dark* " 76
" *He made as though He would have gone further* " . . . 79
" *Take, eat* " 81
" *Trust in the Lord alway* " 83
" *Early my God I bless* " . . . - 85
" *To know . . . the fellowship of His sufferings* " 86
" *He gave thanks* " 88
" *Cast thy burden upon the Lord* " 90
" *Adam, which was the son of God* " 92
" *There shall in no wise enter into it anything that defileth* " 94
" *O let not the Lord be angry, and I will pray but this once* " 95
" *To-day shalt thou be with Me in Paradise* " 97
" *Ye shall be baptized with the Holy Ghost* " 99
" *I am ready to depart* " 101
" *There is a river the streams whereof make glad the city of our God* " 102
" *Man goeth forth to his work and to his labor till the evening* " 104
" *I am the true Vine, and My Father is the Husbandman* " 106

"*Jesus saith unto her, 'Give Me to drink'*" 108

"*Here am I; send* ME" 110

"*Praise the Lord, O my soul*" 114

"*Show me wherefore Thou contendest with me*" 116

"*Thy gentleness hath made me great*" 118

"*Jesus saith unto them, 'Children, have ye any meat?'*" . 120

"*Wilt thou be made whole?*" 121

"*Behold, a king shall reign in righteousness*" 123

"*I will arise*" 125

"*Awake, thou that sleepest, and arise from the dead, and Christ shall give thee light*" 127

"*There was a sound as of a mighty rushing wind, and it filled all the house where they were met*" 129

"*Who shall roll us away the stone from the door of the sepulchre?*" 131

"*Though I walk through the valley of the shadow of death I will fear no evil*" 134

"*Blessed be the Lord for evermore. Amen, and Amen*" . 136

"*Thou thoughtest that I was altogether such an one as thyself*" 138

"*Why stand ye gazing*" 140

"*He first loved us*" 142

"*Where two or three are met together, there am I in the midst of you*" 143

"*Art Thou He that should come?*" 144

"*Verily Thou art a God that hidest Thyself, O God of Israel, the Saviour*" 147

"*He dwelleth* WITH *you and shall be* IN *you*" 150

"*The dove found no rest for the sole of her foot*" . . . 152

"*In my flesh I shall see God*" 154

"*O wretched man that I am! who shall deliver me from the body of this death?*" 155

"*And ye shall take you on the first day, the boughs of goodly trees, branches of palm trees*" 157

" *Listen, O isles, unto Me* " 158

" *Your gold and silver is cankered* " 160

" *O love the Lord* " 162

" *I shall go to him, but he shall not return to me* " 165

" *For Thy name's sake, O Lord, pardon mine iniquity, for it is great* " 167

" *The Lord is my light and my salvation* " 170

" *He was parted from them, and carried up into heaven* " . 172

" *Unto Thee, O Lord, do I lift up my soul* " 174

" *They went forth to meet the Bridegroom* " 176

" *And He said unto him, What is thy name? and he said, Jacob* " 177

" *He doeth all things well* " 180

" *Righteous art Thou, O Lord, when I plead with Thee, yet let me talk with Thee of Thy judgments* " 181

" *O that Ishmael might live before Thee* " 184

" *God is love* " 186

" *If Thou canst believe; all things are possible to him that believeth* " 188

" *Master, where dwellest Thou?* " 190

" *Is it I? and another said, Is it I?* " 193

" *Behold we bring you good tidings* " 195

" *Behold, the Judge standeth at the door* " 198

" *Till Christ be formed in you* " 200

" *Blessed are they that have not seen, and yet have believed* " 202

" *Christ also hath suffered for sins, the just for the unjust, that He might bring us to God, being put to death in the flesh, but quickened by the Spirit: by which also He went and preached unto the spirits in prison; which sometime were disobedient* " 204

NOTES AND EXPLANATIONS 207

Holy Songs, Carols, and Sacred Ballads.

---

*" For none of us liveth to himself, and no man
dieth to himself."*

H E with good gifts that most is blest,
Or stands for God above the rest,
Let him so think — " To serve the dear,
The lowlier children I am here.

" It is the children's bread I break ;
He trusts me with it for their sake ;
(Hunger I must if none it shares)
It is but mine when it is theirs.

" That which I teach, it most is mine,
Dear child of God, to make it thine ;
When thou hast learn'd it, I shall see
The perfect meaning first in thee.

"That song I made it was not mine,
Nor fraught with incense for the shrine,
Till, when thou sang'st it sweetly through,
I with thy voice sang praises too.

"That which I am, it is not mine;
The earth unto the moon doth shine —
Not to herself, for oft her way
Seems but a dark and cloudy day.

"O Church of God! my life is lent
For yours, to spend and to be spent;
O Christ of God! let my death be
Not to myself but Thee — but Thee!"

AMEN.

" Though I take the wings of the morning."

SWEET are His ways who rules above,
  He gives from wrath a sheltering place ;
But covert none is found from grace,
Man shall not hide himself from love.

What though I take to me the wide
  Wings of the morning and forth fly,
  Faster He goes, whose care on high
Shepherds the stars and doth them guide.

What though the tents foregone, I roam
  Till day wax dim lamenting me ;
  He wills that I shall sleep to see
The great gold stairs to His sweet home.

What though the press I pass before,
  And climb the branch, He lifts his face ;
  I am not secret from His grace
Lost in the leafy sycamore.

What though denied with murmuring deep
  I shame my Lord, — it shall not be ;
  For He will turn and look on me,
Then must I think thereon and weep.

The nether depth, the heights above,
  Nor alleys pleach'd of Paradise,
  Nor Herod's judgment-halls suffice :
Man shall not hide himself from love.

"God is the Lord which has showed us light."

SOMEWHERE, quiet in the rest of God,
　　Live our dead, the well-belovèd dead ;
Though we seem'd to leave them 'neath the sod,
　　To the everlasting hills they sped,
　　There they sit, — the well-belovèd dead.

Somewhere, in the counsels known on high,
　　Certain as the southing of a star,
Stands the hour writ down when I shall die.
　　O to go where all my good things are,
　　Calmly as the southing of a star.

Somewhere, safely hidden, lost in light,
　　Our good country lies — Immanuel's land ;
Earn'd for us and soon to bless our sight.
　　Anchor'd fast to God, a radiant strand,
　　O my heart's desire — Immanuel's land.

"I have loved thee with an everlasting love."

DEAR is the lost wife to a lone man's heart,
    When in a dream he meets her at his door,
And, waked for joy, doth know she dwells apart,
    All unresponsive on a silent shore ;
Dearer, yea, more desired art thou — for thee
My divine heart yearns by the jasper sea.

More than the mother's for her sucking child ;
    She wants, with emptied arms and love untold,
Her most dear little one that on her smiled
    And went ; but more, I want Mine own. Behold,
I long for My redeem'd, where safe with Me
Twelve manner of fruits grow on th' immortal tree ;

The tree of life that I won back for men,
    And planted in the city of My God.
Lift up thy head, I love thee ; wherefore, then,
    Liest thou so long on thy memorial sod
Sleeping for sorrow ? Rise, for dawn doth break —
I love thee, and I cry to thee " Awake."

Serve, — woman whom I love, ere noon be high,
   Ere the long shadow lengthen at thy feet.
Work, — I have many poor, O man, that cry,
   My little ones do languish in the street.
Love, — 'tis a time for love, since I love thee.
Live, — 'tis a time to live. Man, live in Me.

"*And fell on his neck, and kissed him.*"

THOU wert far off, and in the sight of heaven
    Dead.   And thy Father would not this should
        be ;
And now thou livest, it is all forgiven ;
    Think on it, O my soul, He kissèd thee !

What now are gold and gear? thou canst afford
    To cast them from thee at His sacred call,
As Mary, when she met her living Lord,
    The burial spice she had prepared let fall.

O ! what is death to life?   One dead could well
    Afford to waste his shroud, if he might wake ;
Thou canst afford to waste the world, and sell
    Thy footing in it, for the new world's sake.

What is the world? it is a waiting place,
    Where men put on their robes for that above.
What is the new world? 'tis a Father's face
    Beholden of His sons — the face of love.

CHRISTMAS HYMN.

"Let us now go even unto Bethlehem."

O NIGHT of nights! O night
    Desired of man so long!
The ancient heavens fled forth in light
    To sing thee thy new song;
And shooting down the steep,
    To shepherd folk of old,
An angel, while they watch'd their sheep,
    Set foot beside the fold.

Lo! while as like to die
    Of that keen light he shed,
They look'd on his pure majesty,
    Amazed, and sore bestead;
Lo! while with words of cheer
    He bade their trembling cease,
The flocks of God swept sweetly near,
    And sang to them of peace.

All on the hillside grass
  That fulgent radiance fell,
So close those innocents did pass,
  Their words were heard right well ;
Among the sheep, their wings
  Some folding, walk'd the sod
An order'd throng of shining things,
  White, with the smile of God.

The waits of heaven to hear,
  Oh! what it must have been !
Think, Christian people, think, and fear
  For cold hearts, for unclean ;
Think how the times go by,
  How love and longing fail,
Think how we live and how we die,
  As this were but a tale.

O tender tale of old,
  Live in thy dear renown ;
God's smile was in the dark, behold
  That way His hosts came down ;
Light up, great God, Thy Word,
  Make the blest meaning strong,
As if our ears, indeed, had heard
  The glory of their song.

It was so far away,
　　But Thou could'st make it near,
And all its living might display
　　And cry to it, " Be here,"
Here, in th' unresting town,
　　As once remote to them,
Who heard it when the heavens came down,
　　On pastoral Bethlehem.

It was so long ago,
　　But God can make it *now*,
And as with that sweet overflow,
　　Our empty hearts endow;
Take, Lord, those words outworn,
　　O ! make them new for aye,
Speak — " Unto you a child is born,"
　　To-day — to-day — to-day.

" Blessed are ye that weep now."

WEEPING and wailing needs must be
    When Love His name shall disavow,
When christen'd men His wrath shall dree,
Who mercy scorn'd in this their day;
But what?　He turns not yet away,
    Not yet — not now.

Let me not, waken'd after sleep,
    Behold a Judge with lowering brow,
The world must weep, and I must weep
Those sins that nail'd Thee on the tree,
Lord Jesu, of Thy clemency,
    Let it be Now.

Let us have weeping Now for sin,
    And not us only; let Thy tears
Avail the tears of many to win;
Weep with us, Jesu, kind art Thou;
We that have sinn'd many long years,
    Let us weep Now;

And then, waked up, behold Thy face,
  Who did forgive us. See Thy brow —
Beautiful — learn Thy love and grace.
Then wilt Thou wipe away our tears,
And comfort in th' all-hallow'd spheres,
  Them that weep now.

MORNING.

" The Lord our God is one Lord."

GOD, to men Thy children shown
    A Creator on the throne,
A Redeemer for them given,
A Renewer come from heaven ;

God, the night and day are Thine,
God, my fathers' God and mine ;
Now with dawn the East is fair,
Hearken to my morning prayer.

God in heaven, and God in me,
Let me serve in my degree
As the sun ; and let me love
As the seraphim above.

Since Thou waitest me to bless,
I will ask Thee nothing less ;
Let Thy likeness wax alway
In my soul as dawn to day.

Let my work be alway done
As to Thee, and when the sun
Sets and all Thy stars appear,
Still acquaint me I am dear.

Though so many and so far,
Thou dost know them, every star
By its name — O ! life divine,
God, Thou also knowest mine.

In Thy one appointed way,
Pardon for my sins I pray,
In the great name ever blest,
Ask Thee for the most and best.

Our Father, dread and wise,
Our redeeming Sacrifice,
Our Renewer, let me be
Satisfied, at last, in Thee.

"*Behold the man.*"

THOU hast found me and I faint, I cannot bear
    Thy light ;
I have eaten of the bitter bread of sin ;
I have said, " There is no hope," I am vile in God's
    sight ;
I would cleanse me, but O how shall I begin ?

My eternal Father, Thy great gift I despised ;
    Of a broken heart He is dying, His head droops
      low ; —
O, one more day of grace, thou Saviour sacrificed ;
    O, one more call, I — whither shall I go ?

My crime to me comes home — the Judge is at the
    door —
The voice of my Brother's blood doth on me call ;
I cannot wash me clean with tears for evermore,
    Yet my stains are in His sight who seeth all.

Now he is made my slayer, this my Saviour slain —
    Slain from the world's foundation He me ac-
      cuseth ; —
Lord Christ, upon the cross how long wilt Thou remain,
    Pierced for the doomèd world that Thee refuseth ?

Better, better for me, than such a day should be,
  Falling rocks and mountains should a grave af-
    ford ;
Where shall I safety find? whither shall I flee?
  Where hide my guilty head from the suffering Lord?

Words from a dying mouth, love's strange admonish-
    ment
  "Go not — nay, come, take hold on the deadly tree,
Here seek where thou art sought — to thy peace con-
    sent,
  Thou canst not covert find — thou art found of Me.

"Slain, and of thee ; thy life stands in My death re-
    veal'd.
  Look unto Me, lost soul, look ! thou shalt not die ;
Thy sins have nail'd Me here — here is thy pardon
    seal'd :
  None other can forgive, lo, I forgive, even I."

" What aileth thee, Hagar ? '

RISE, for God calls thee, leaning down to bless,
     Aye to thy tears attent ;
Why sitt'st thou, dying of drought all shelterless,
Mourning, like Hagar in the wilderness,
     When the water was spent.

The river of Egypt she did think upon,
     Whereof she drank of yore.
But she did thirst again. The white sun shone
Blinding above her head — her strength was gone —
     The bondwoman hoped no more.

Then she lift up her voice and wept, and He
     Above did audience give.
He call'd her. Rise, for so He calls to thee,
Opens thine eyes a well of water to see —
     Drink, desolate soul, and live.

Water of Life ! God's gift to man's distress,
     When he lamenting sore
Doth mourn like Hagar in the wilderness ;
Behold it, flowing and free, His love confess,
     Drink thou, and thirst no more.

*" Let my prayer come before Thee: incline Thine ear
unto my cry."*

NOW the psalm to heaven ascending,
   Sighs of heart are with it blending;
Close together, all unknown,
Each from each doth stand alone.
Nothing of our grief we tell,
Nay, but, God, Thou knowest it well;
Each from Thee for comfort seeks,
In whose ear the silence speaks.

Is it poverty?   He knoweth,
In whose light the hid thing showeth;
Straighten'd measure, endless care,
Hard for them we love to bear
Left behind in life's great plan,
Seeking not for aid from man,
Thou the want, the strife canst see,
The poor commends himself to Thee.

Is it sorrow?   God, He knoweth,
Up to whom the sighing goeth ;
Yea, He knoweth, who doth bless,
Yet not spare its bitterness.
I, in sorrow, pain, and loss,
Kiss with many tears the cross ;
Tears are my meat: comfort Thou me,
My tears commend themselves to Thee.

Is it sin?   Good Lord, Thou knowest ;
My dark places Thou me showest ;
Though Thy mercy hold me fast,
Nothing can undo the past:
I repent me of my ways ;
I go softly all my days ;
My sinful soul doth only flee —
Doth still commend itself to Thee.

Lend Thy wings, immortal Dove,
Bear our wants, our tears above.
Live, Thou Lord that didst atone,
Great High Priest, before the throne ;
Little of our griefs we tell,
Thou, O Father, knowest them well ;
Each from Thee may comfort seek,
In whose ear doth silence speak.

" If any man will come to Me, and hate not . . . his own life also, he cannot be My disciple."

LET me hate mine own life,
　　That I led in evil ways;
Envy, lying, lust, and strife,
　　Selfish nights and careless days.

Mine own life, I knew not
　　It was death; but now 'tis meet
It were buried, hid, forgot;—
　　Christ, I lay it at Thy feet.

Let me lose mine own life
　　For Thy sake, and put on Thine;
Though it be with dangers rife,
　　In the ending it shall shine.

Mine own life — lay it low;
　　Let me Thy disciple be;
Bear Thy cross, and even so
　　Live to God, and rest in Thee.

"I am poor and needy, yet the Lord heareth me."

WHEN children are sick, when times are hard,
    (Lord, Christ, hear on Thy heavenly shore)
Thou to my sighing dost lend regard,
    For God is my God for evermore.

In the burden and heat of the day,
    (Lord, Christ, hear on Thy heavenly shore)
Oft am I troubled, and scarce can pray,
    But God is my God for evermore.

When I lie, bound of my sins, and cry,
    (Lord, Christ, hear on Thy heavenly shore)
Thou wilt me pity, I shall not die,
    For God is my God for evermore.

In wint'ry weather, when I'm grown old,
    (Lord, Christ, hear on Thy heavenly shore)
Thy comforts cheer me, though nights be cold,
    And God is my God for evermore.

White as hoar-frost is my bow'd head,
   (Lord, Christ, hear on Thy heavenly shore)
Though I can earn me nor warmth nor bread,
   My God is my God for evermore.

My strength faileth, my heart beats low,
   (Lord, Christ, hear on Thy heavenly shore)
I must leave you, my friends — I must go,
   But God is my God for evermore.

" Behold, I stand at the door."

ALL desiring, nothing won,
    Man, thy day is nearly done;
Is the path of life begun?

Ere its waning hour be o'er,
Call this poor soul once, once more,
Jesu standing at the door.

Knock, but, O! most patient Lord,
Strength to open first afford;
Will to grasp love's sweet award.

Man, He standeth yet full fain,
Let not, let not all be vain;
Take the everlasting gain.

Open, bid Him in, and fall
At His feet, who doth thee call;
In His mercy stands thine all.

Weeping, kiss the sacred feet,
Thorn-crown'd King, Thine eyes are sweet;
Master, is it thus we meet?

Lord, dost Thou remember me?
Lord, I nail'd Thee on the tree ;
Lord, good Lord, I scoff'd at Thee !

O ! my sins against me cry ;
O ! my guilt is deep and high ; —
" Peace," He saith, " thou shalt not die.

" Peace, peace — all those sins of thine
I have wash'd in blood divine ;
I forgive thee — thou art Mine."

CAROL.

WITH A BURDEN.

"And there were shepherds."

OVER the long green downs, when I do wander
　　After the ewes and lambs, so oft I ponder,
" When the Chief Shepherd comes, that is full tender,
He will, of all His own, true reckoning render;
Them that give suck and feed, them from dust raisèd;
Praise the good Lord, therefore."
　　　　　　　　　　　　　　The Lord be praisèd.

When 'tis a darksome night, and deep snow drifteth,
When many lambs are lost ere the storm lifteth,
I think, " When Thou shalt come, though the dark
　　　blind me,
Lord, 'twill be light to Thee, straight Thou wilt find me;
I, when Thou call'st my soul, with light amazèd
Shall in Thy light see light."
　　　　　　　　　　　　　　The Lord be praisèd.

Oft as the day comes round, this drear December,
How shepherds sat of old, still I remember,
And Thou didst send them news, straight from Thy
    city,
All of Thy great good-will and Thy dear pity ;
Glad were the shepherds then with glory dazèd ;
Praise the good Lord, therefòre.

                    The Lord be praisèd.

Sing, O thou favoured earth,

                    The Lord be praisèd.

Sing, for thy Saviour's birth,

                    The Lord be praisèd.

Heaven shall not hold Him long ;

                    The Lord be praisèd.

For prayers of love are strong,

                    The Lord be praisèd.

Thy star shall shine again,   ·

                    The Lord be praisèd.

Thy King come back to reign.

                    The Lord be praisèd.

SONG OF PRAISE FOR LONDON.

WITH A CHORUS.

" Praise is comely."

ON Zion's hill the sacred dust
　　Lies bare 'neath arid skies ;
From ruin'd walls her sons are thrust,
　　Foregone her sacrifice.
But Zion's voice lives yet; and brought
　　Adown the ages ring
The songs of praise he sweetly taught
　　That was her shepherd king.

O King David ! King David sang of old
Among the little water'd valleys while he watch'd the
　　fold ;
Over rocks of wild En-gedi when he sheathed the
　　sword :
And would we had King David's harp, and so could
　　praise the Lord !

" I will give thanks, my God, O King,
    And of Thy goodness tell ;
Upon the heights of Zion sing
    Thou Hope of Israel.
The hill of Zion is right fair —
    A city of great fame ;
For why ? The Lord our God is there,
    Excellent is His name.

" Ye tribes that in His courts have stood,
    Ye priests that on Him wait,
O praise the Lord, for He is good,
    And only He is great.
Praise Him, thou great, thou lesser light,
    That toil and sleep control ;
Praise Him, you angels in the height;
    Praise the Lord, O my soul."

O King David ! King David on his throne
And under murmurous cedars making dusks on Leb-
    anon,
And by the Jordan's sailless waters sang full sweet
    and clear :
And though King David's harp be mute, let us sing
    praises HERE.

For somewhat aye that moves and yearns
   To all things just and free ;
For many a soul that inly burns
   More righteous days to see ;
For peace, for law, for gold, for wheat,
   And for His printed word,
Praise Him, ye throngs in every street ;
   Great London, praise the Lord.

Ye that her bridges cross by night,
   Where on the river play
A thousand stars from lamps alight,
   That mete out narrower day,
Praise Him, and say this river bears
   Great fleets that ceaseless go ;
And yet, for these eight hundred years
   Hath not borne in a foe.

Praise Him, great city fair and free,
   And helpless, but for God ;
Nor siege, nor sack have frighted thee,
   Of alien hosts untrod.
Praise Him, and pray while yet 'tis well,
   Nor danger nigh thee waits ;
Pray thy Celestial Sentinel
   To guard thy silver gates.

Praise Him, when clash thy weighty hours
   By measure night and day ;
Praise Him, while yet a hundred towers
   Ring out thy times to pray.
Praise Him, where murmurous fall and swell
   (As of some wind-borne chord)
The majesty of millions tell ;
   Great London, praise the Lord !

O King David ! King David's harp rang true ;
But we have learn'd a wondrous song King David
   never knew.
To One was born of David's line, sing high with sweet
   accord ;
For One who died that we might live, great London,
   praise the Lord !

CHRISTMAS WAITS.

" We bring you good tidings."

FIRST PART.

G OD'S great Gift to man forlorn,
   In a winter night was born ;
Angels tell the glorious tale,
Let not, earth, thy welcome fail.
   "All hail," and "all hail."

Little child, how sunk Thy lot !
Thy great might Thou hast forgot ;
Guider of all stars that shone,
Sleep, Thy glory is clean gone.
   Sleep on, and sleep on.

Wake, you friends and neighbours, wake,
And thank God for this Child's sake ;
Sing, my heart, the anthem swell,
Since that blessèd birth befell,
   All's well, and all's well.

Now is won the gift that we
Lost beneath the apple-tree,
Now is won the heavenly shore,
Where light wanes, and life gives o'er
    No more, and no more.

SECOND PART.

God's great Gift to creatures vile
Was not welcomed long, erewhile,
Soon they sent Him home, and He
Through the gates of death did flee.
    Ah me, and ah me !

But, in love He came and went,
For His kindness was not spent,
Now His merits aye prevail
Where no more the welcomes fail.
    " All hail," and " all hail !"

He went up to His own place,
We, ere long, shall see His face,
Forty — thirty — twenty — ten
Years, or days, Christ Jesus then.
    Amen, and amen.

" The time of the singing of birds is come."

THICK orchards, all in white,
    Stand 'neath blue voids of light,
And birds among the branches blithely sing,
    For they have all they know ;
    There is no more, but so,
All perfectness of living, fair delight of spring.

    Only the cushat dove
    Makes answer as for love
To the deep yearning of man's yearning breast ;
    And mourneth, to his thought,
    As in her notes were wrought
Fulfill'd in her sweet having, sense of his unrest.

    Not with possession, not
    With fairest earthly lot,
Cometh the peace assured, his spirit's quest ;
    With much it looks before,
    With most it yearns for more ;
And 'this is not our rest,' and 'this is not our rest.'

Give Thou us more.   We look
For more.   The heart that took
All spring-tide for itself were empty still ;
    Its yearning is not spent
    Nor silenced in content,
Till He that all things filleth doth it sweetly fill.

Give us Thyself.   The May
Dureth so short a day ;
Youth and the spring are over all too soon ;
    Content us while they last,
    Console us for them past,
Thou with whom bides for ever life, and love, and noon.

FROM PSALM CXXX.

" OUT of the deep, out of the deep,
    O God, I make my moan ;
When I by night awaked from sleep
    Do watch with Thee alone.

" Be not extreme, be not extreme
    To mark what is amiss ;
Forgiveness doth Thee well beseem —
    Lord, be Thou fear'd in this.

" My soul doth wait, my soul doth wait
    Till darkness wear away;
My soul doth flee, I say, to Thee
    Before the breaking day.

" Trust in the Lord, trust in the Lord,
    Though yet thy dawn be dim ;
He will thee save from out the grave,
    Redemption is with him."

" If we be dead with Him, we shall also live with Him."

I AM dead with Thee, and I remain
    Buried, dark beneath the covering clod ;
In my heart, O Master, rise again,
    And ascend, as in my sight, to God.

In that great way draw me up and guide ;
  . Tell my soul Thou wilt not her forsake ;
While I follow, near to me abide,
    Else O how shall I that journey make ?

It is long as life, and I am weak ;
    It is great, as all Thy counsels tell ;
Very glorious, high and far to seek
    Lies the goal, — O gird me for it well.

All my burdens I must cast on Thee.
    Use my riches for Thyself, and wear
Thou mine honours.   Jesu, bear for me
    My deep griefs, and carry, Lord, my care.

Now must I set forth, nor doubt, nor wait,
  Great Forerunner to Thy glory pass'd ;
Thou hast pardon'd ; through the golden gate
  O receive me to Thy home at last.

" *Come unto Me.*"

IT is the Lord.   He stands with thorny crown
   That I did help to press upon His brow.
Is mine a lost soul?   Nay; for He looks down
   In love upon me sunk into the slough
Of my despond, and calls — O, can it be? —
     "Come unto Me!"

"This unkind world, which promised all and gave
   Nothing, thou long hast served it, and for nought;
But now thou knowest its glory cannot save,
   Nor its grace comfort.   One there is takes thought
Upon thy grief.   Myself have pitied thee, —
     Come unto Me!

"O thou deceived, and wounded, and cast by,
   Now in thy poverty, distress, despair,
Emptied of good, look on thy hope — come nigh;
   So look away thy misery and thy care,
Thou yet shall have enough and all good see —
     Come unto Me!

"Come with thy yearning void, thy deep unrest,
  And all thy sins and thy deplorèd shame ;
For I can wash thee clean and clear thy breast,
  That knoweth not yet its Great Want's greater
    name,
My name, even Mine.   Behold, I wait for thee ! —
    Come unto Me ! "

"And I said, Oh that I had wings like a dove."

O ! THAT I had wings,
Then would I flee away and be at rest ;
I would go up where rapt the seraph sings,
There would I satisfy my soul oppress'd,
In the white peace above ;
And lay me at the feet of God's great love.
O ! that I had wings
Like a dove.

Trembling cometh over me ;
They whom Thou hast died to free,
Bind ; whom Thou hast loved, despise ; —
Aliens each in other's eyes.

O ! that bitter words might cease,
That my portion might be peace ;
O ! that love Thy Church might bless,
While she walks this wilderness.

Woe is me for hate and scorn,
Wounding stings of envy born ;
When the kneeling saint doth scoff,
What shall be the end thereof ?

4

Woe is me, because they meet,
Ay, and strive at Thine own feet
At Thy cross, for us who bled
Saviour; and I said, I said, —

O! that I had wings,
Then would I flee away and be at rest,
I would go up where rapt the seraph sings,
There would I satisfy my soul oppress'd,
     In the white peace above;
And lay me at the feet of God's great love;
     O! that I had wings
         Like a dove.

ADVENT SUNDAY. EVENING.

" What I say unto you I say unto all, Watch."

"WATCHMAN, what of the night?"
 "An hour is struck on high,
But yet is no streak of light
 In the solemn, starless sky;
Dark nor the dayspring breaketh,
 The world is drowsed and dumb;
I sleep, but my heart waketh;
 When will the Bridegroom come?"

"He is gone up, O bride,
 His Father's smile to see;
The wound is heal'd in His side,
 He plants, for thy sake, a tree;
Thy speech on His tongue rings sweet,
 His country is plain to view,
For He brought its dust on His feet,
 His locks were wet with dew."

" Wind of the South, awake !
   And thou, O North wind, blow !
Move in my garden, and make
   All my chief spices flow ;
Bud, and bud, in the night,
   Fruitful tree and fair flower,
Till, with shocks of instant light,
   Sounds forth the Bridegroom's hour.

" I have fed on holy food,
   Thou breakest me bread divine ;
The wine of Thy cup is good,
   But Thy love is better than wine.
Lord, when Thou comest to sup,
   I shall know how this can be,
For Thyself shall hold the cup,
   I shall drink of it new with Thee.

" Grant me, O Christ, the grace,
   That present love to greet ;
Fain would I see Thy face,
   And lie at Thy sacred feet ;
Fain would I hear Thy voice
   Speak the language of men ;
Then shall Thy bride rejoice,
   Then, O never, till then."

" Rise up, O bride, in the night,
    Take thy lamp, and take oil,
Put on thy raiment white
    The Bridegroom took for a spoil ;
Prepare, let thy feet be shod,
    For thy heart doth prophesy
Thy desire is born of God,
    And is made thy destiny."

" Consider the lilies of the field."

WHEN through the meads I go,
    Or where Lent-lilies blow,
Or purple pasque-flowers, and primroses pale ;
    I think they look'd e'en so,
    When my Lord lived below ;
So in their month made sweet the chosen vale.

    All tender and all mild,
    A little two-years' child,
He mark'd them trembling on the slender stem.
    Sweet Innocent! and He
    Did stoop, it well may be,
Right pleased, as other babes, to gather them.

    Emptied, as was His will,
    Who erst did all things fill,
The Lord that made them knew them not by name ;
    The speech of heaven foregone,
    Not yet had learn'd our tongue,
And pluck'd with inarticulate sweet acclaim.

Lord, when I stand and gaze
On the night heavens, Thy ways
Confound my thought, they are too great for me ;
But wonders, these are none,
Thou hast them so outdone
In the great ways of Thy humility.

"In Him we live, and move, and have our being."

THE measureless gulfs of air are full of Thee :
    Thou Art, and therefore hang the stars ; they
         wait,
And swim, and shine in God who bade them be,
    And hold their sundering voids inviolate.

A God concern'd (veil'd in pure light) to bless,
    With sweet revealing of His love, the soul ;
Toward things piteous, full of piteousness ;
    The Cause, the Life, and the continuing Whole.

He is more present to all things He made[1]
    Than anything unto itself can be ;
Full-foliaged boughs of Eden could not shade
    Afford, since God was also 'neath the tree.

Thou knowest me altogether ; I knew not
    Thy likeness till Thou mad'st it manifest.
There is no world but is Thy heaven ; no spot
    Remote ; Creation leans upon Thy breast.

Thou art beyond all stars, yet in my heart
    Wonderful whisperings hold Thy creature dumb ;
I need no search afar ; to me Thou art
    Father, Redeemer, and Renewer — come.

              [1] Note 1.

A PORTION OF PSALM XLII.

"As the hart panteth."

AS the hart panteth, fainting;—and forward looks,
　　Urged over the desert wilds, and sultry lea;
As the hart panteth after the water brooks,
　　So panteth my soul after Thee.

My soul is athirst for God — the living God;
　　When shall I come and appear, O God, before Thee?
When I remember how I Thy courts have trod,
　　I pour out my soul in me.

I went with the multitude, with joy and praise,
　　With such as keep holiday; but lo! my crown
Is trod in the dust, I mourn through all my days;
　　O my God, my soul is cast down.

Tears are my meat, yet upward my spirit looks;
　　Though Thou me slay, Thou only my hope shalt be;
As the hart panteth after the water brooks,
　　So panteth my soul after Thee.

"*Lord, what is man?*"

WHEN it was well with me,
    Oft I sent up to Thee
My heart in prayer;
Now I lie frail and faint,
Send I my sad complaint,
    Where art Thou — where?

Answer me, else undone,
Holy and mighty One,
    With glory shod;
Searching the starry weft,
Thy garment's hem — bereft
    I feel for God.

But Thy great host doth all
Moving, majestical,
    Heaven's outwork span;
Lord, what is this I see?
They are too high for me;
    Lord, what is man?

Yet Thou didst visit him
Set at creation's rim ;
   Thou hast been here ;
Where Thou hast been, Thou art,
Thou hast nor past, nor part,
   Nor far, nor near.

Thou art all — now — before —
Thy time is evermore
   Set at to-day ;
Thy Spirit, Lord, doth brood
Yet o'er the waters rude,
   Forming for aye.

God, since Thou changest not
Now is made fair my lot,
   Though I be dust ;
Maker, redeeming Lord,
Spirit of grace, afford
   Me a sure trust.

Let me not doubt nor fear,
Man had Thy own Son here,
   Pledge of all grace ;
Teach me on earth His love,
Then in Thy house above,
   Show me His face.

" Ye also, as lively stones, are built up a spiritual house."

SUCH as have not gold to bring Thee,
    They bring thanks — Thy grateful sons ;
Such as have no song to sing Thee,
    Live Thee praise — Thy silent ones.

Such as have their unknown dwelling,
    Secret from Thy children here,
Known of Thee, will Thee be telling
    How Thy ways with them are dear.

None the place ordained refuseth,
    They are one, and they are all
Living stones, the Builder chooseth
    For the courses of His wall.

Now Thy work by us fulfilling,
    Build us in Thy house divine ;
Each one cries, "I, Lord, am willing,
    Whatsoever place be mine."

Some, of every eye beholden,
  Hewn to fitness for the height,
By Thy hand to beauty moulden,
  Show Thy workmanship in light.

Other, Thou dost bless with station
  Dark, and of the foot downtrod,
Sink them deep in the foundation —
  Buried, hid with Christ in God.

I.

" He made the stars also."

WHEN the ardent sun rides high,
    Then the uncorrupt pure blue
Shows itself a worldless sky ;
    Children, thus it shows to you.

When the sun withdraws his light,
    Lo ! the stars of God are there ;
Present hosts unseen till night —
    Matchless, countless, silent, fair.

Children, oft when joy shines clear
    Lost is hold of hope divine ;
Then the night of grief draws near,
    And God's countless comforts shine.

As its darkness deep outbars
    All things else they start to view ;
Mercies, countless as the stars —
    Matchless, changeless, perfect, true.

II.

" He hath put the world in their hearts."

AS the veil of broidery fine
    For the temple wrought of old,
Dropp'd before the awful shrine,
    Bloom'd in purple, gleam'd in gold ;

So the broider'd earth and sky,
    Ever present, always near,
Charm the soul and fill the eye —
    Marvellous, matchless, beauteous, dear.

While the veil our God hath wrought
    Hangs before the holy place,
It must reign o'er sight and thought,
    Drawn between us and His face.

When the veil is rent in twain
    Shall the present God appear ;
We shall see Him then full fain —
    Matchless, changeless, perfect, fair.

" Surely the bitterness of death is past."

I T is not dying daunts the heart, •
   Who die to God forget the smart;
The sick full oft draw painful breath,
Yet, fear no bitterness of death —
No, 'tis the want the needy feel,
And their disgrace, whom none can heal ;
Their anguish sore that walk in strife —
It is the bitterness of life.

Thou hast spoil'd death, Lord, of renown :
Man's life by man lies trodden down,
And who can lift his heart to Thee,
And swear, " of this guilt I am free "? •
The darts by lost Apollyon hurl'd,
The weight, the labouring of the world,
These are not ours to bear, yet we
Have sinn'd in Thy sight, verily, —

We and our fathers — we are nought,
So the world's woe transcends our thought ;

But make us wise of heart and true,
The right to learn, the right to do ;
For heaven Thy Church aspires and faints,
Sweet is the death, Lord, of Thy saints ;
But teach them here to aid the strife,
And soothe the bitterness of life.

5

" And He carried me away in the spirit to a great and high mountain, and showed me that great city, the holy Jerusalem."

WHEN I lie waking, my heart nigh to breaking,
　　When all things are dark and cold ;
When my bread faileth, and fear assaileth
　　Me, a sinner grown sick, grown old ;
When no man careth how with me it fareth,
　　For no soul doth count me dear ;
Poor, hungry, sighing, a life most like dying,
　　And no nest in any tree here ;
I think on that dwelling all sweet homes excelling,
　　And long there entrance to win.
O fair, fair city ! Christ, for Thy pity,
　　　　Call this poor exile in.

There is no earning with sore work nor learning,
　　A welcome its peace to share ;
My God, so be it.　I should never see it,
　　If the cost were my cost to bear ;
My misery showeth, and well Thy heart knoweth
　　Nought have I wherewith to pay :
Nought ; and no merit, who would fain inherit
　　That city more fair than the day,

Where no want fretteth, where the soul forgetteth,
  Fed with manna, the bitter bread of sin.
O most fair city! Christ, for Thy pity,
      Call this poor exile in.

O most sweet gladness, slipt away from sadness
  To rest in the long release,
Pluck leaves of healing, and, safe with God's sealing,
  Under the palm-trees have peace.
Hear blameless angels sing their sweet evangels ;
  Behold kneeling saints in the way
Where, unreprovèd, for one well-belovèd,
  They wait in the cool of the day.
O most fair dwelling, all sweet homes excelling,
  Thy beauty fain would I win.
O most dear city ! Christ, for Thy pity,
      Call this poor exile in.

GOOD FRIDAY.

" There was darkness."

A MORN of guilt, an hour of doom —
　　Shocks and tremblings dread ;
All the city sunk in gloom —
　　Thick darkness overhead.
An awful Sufferer straight and stark ;
　　Mocking voices fell ;
Tremblings — tremblings in the dark,
　　In heaven, and earth, and hell.

Groping, stumbling up the way,
　　They pass, whom Christ forgave ;
They know not what they do — they say,
　　" Himself He cannot save.
On His head behold the crown
　　That alien hands did weave ;
Let Him come down, let Him come down,
　　And we will believe ! "

Fearsome dreams, a rending veil,
　　Cloven rocks down hurl'd ;
God's love itself doth seem to fail
　　The Saviour of the world.
Dying thieves do curse and wail,
　　Either side is scorn ;
Lo ! He hangs while some cry " Hail ! "
　　Of heaven and earth forlorn.

Still o'er His passion darkness lowers,
　　He nears the deathly goal ;
But He shall see in His last hours
　　Of the travail of His soul ;
'Lo, a cry ! — the firstfruits given
　　On the accursèd tree —
" Dying Love of God in heaven,
　　Lord, remember me ! "

By His sacrifice, foreknown
　　Long ages ere that day,
And by God's sparing of His own
　　Our debt of death to pay ;
By the Comforter's consent,
　　With ardent flames bestow'd,
In this dear race when Jesus went
　　To make His mean abode —

By the pangs God look'd not on,
   And the world dared not see ;
By all redeeming wonders won
   Through that dread mystery ; —
Lord, receive once more the sigh
   From the accursèd tree —
" Sacred Love of God most high,
   O remember me !"

FRIDAY.

"It was the eve of the Sabbath."

AS on this day the Lamb, the Sacrifice,
   Gave up His breath and closed His darkening
      eyes ;
As on this day within the tomb was laid, —
   Consider it, my soul, and be afraid.

And say not thou, " He died, and it is done,"
   For yet He dieth for man — th' Eternal Son ;
Slain first, the Lord of life, when death came in,
   And Eve put forth her hand to her first sin.

Then Christ, who was her life, died in her soul,
   And still dies daily as the ages roll.
Albeit a way He found to raise us more
   And set man higher than he was before.

And was it once — but once — the King of Love,
   To save the lost, forsook His home above?
Perhaps, e'en now, some other world astray
   Beholds His death and hews His grave to-day.

O Thou that gavest all, I would receive
   All at Thy hand, and tremble and believe
Thou dost me clear of guilt, great Father, make ;
   Now would I loathe my sins for Thy Son's sake.

I ask Thee not a lenient God to be ;
   Rather to make mé what Thou lov'st to see ;
Then look upon me in my Head, and know
   What goodness and what grace once lived below.

I also look on Him as one full fain
   To grow into His likeness — to attain,
Reflected from His face some ray divine,
   Caught of that pureness which doth round Him
      shine.

Albeit the copy be so faint, so dim,
   Yet one day I shall truly be like Him ;
And all my heart's desire and all my prayer
   Is at His feet to lie, and thank Thee there.

Double Hymn.

" They went and made the sepulchre sure, sealing the stone and setting a watch."

I.

WHO shall begin the wondrous, wondrous story?
    Tell how the Lord is dead — the Lord of
        glory?
With reverent fear approach the sealèd stone,
And mourn because of Him that lyeth alone?

I.

We will begin the wondrous, wondrous story.
They left Him in His tomb — the Lord of glory —
Enwrapp'd with myrrh and spices of the dead,
And linen swathed about His sacred head.

Love's denied King. Behold Him! watch one hour
Beneath His closèd lids the death-shades lower,
On His cold shroud cold costly balms distil,
And the cold healing hands lie still, lie still.

2.

Who shall go on? The Father loved Him well.
Did He come down and enter? None can tell.
O wondrous mystery! for man too deep ;
The Christ is dead no more, He lyeth asleep.

2.

We will go on, with reverent, reverent fear.
After the blanks of death our Saviour dear,
It may be, shrouded yet, in saintly peace
Gave thanks to God because of man's release,

And knew He lived again and will'd to wake,
Whisper'd the sealèd stone and bade it break ;
When, like a flash of lightning fall'n from heaven,
An angel answer'd as the word was given.

Behold the Roman guard in dread affright
Flee from the quaking rocks, the dazzling light ;
And other angels light on His cold floor,
And minister, and marvel, and adore.

3.

Who may go on with this so marvellous thing,
Love's suffering, dying, living Lord to sing?
One to the night comes forth. Behold ! 'tis He
Clad in His robes of immortality.

3.

Since He was man — then man may think as man —
He breathed a conscious calm ere joy began ;
A rapture of deep rest that nothing saith,
New from the cold solemnities of death.

Haply fulfill'd of peace He stood alone,
And all God's love came on Him from the throne ;
The hovering mystic Dove, it may be, fell
Upon the breast of our Immanuel.

4.

But none can, none can tell the marvellous story,
The thoughts of Christ, the living Lord of glory ;
Since He was God, my God foreknew His reign,
That Light of light would shine in light again.

Since He was man, the warmèd night-air dim,
The garden odours warm were sweet to Him ;
And warmèd world, beneath whose bowers withdrawn,
He waited for His mourners till the dawn,

And said to them, " All hail ! " — O, greeting sweet,
The kneeling women hold Him by the feet.
Heaven's gates fly open.   So His words prevail,
That earth for ever answers, " Hail, all hail ! "

" *While it was yet dark.*"

MARY of Magdala, when the moon had set,
  Forth to the garden that was with night dews
    wet,
Fared in the dark — woe-wan and bent was she,
'Neath many pounds' weight of fragrant spicery.

Mary of Magdala, in her misery,
" Who shall roll the stone up from yon door ? " quoth
    she ;
And trembling down the steep she went, and wept sore,
Because her dearest Lord was, alas ! no more.

Her burden she let fall, lo ! the stone was gone ;
Light was there within, out to the dark it shone ;
With an angel's face the dread tomb was bright,
The which she beholding fell for sore affright.

Mary of Magdala, in her misery,
Heard the white vision speak, and did straightway
    flee ;
And an idle tale seem'd the wild words she said,
And nought her heart received — nought was com-
    forted.

"Nay" quoth the men He loved, when they came to
    see,
"Our eyes beheld His death, the Saint of Galilee;
Who have borne Him hence truly we cannot say;"
Secretly in fear, they turn'd and went their way.

Mary of Magdala, in her misery,
Follow'd to the tomb, and wept full bitterly,
Linger'd in the dark, where first the Lord was laid;
The white one spake again, she was no more afraid.

In a moment — dawn! solemn, and sweet, and clear,
Kneeling, yet she weeps, and some one stands anear;
Asketh of her grief — she, all her thoughts are dim,
"If thou hast borne Him hence, tell me," doth an-
    swer Him.

"Mary," He saith, no more, shades of night have
    fled
Under dewy leaves, behold Him! — death is dead;
"Mary," and "O my Master," sorrow speeds away,
Sunbeams touch His feet this earliest Easter day.

After the pains of death, in a place unknown,
Trembling, of visions haunted, and all alone,
I too shall want Thee, Jesus, my hope, my trust,
Fall'n low, and all unclothed, even of my poor dust.

I, too, shall hear Thee speak, Jesus, my life divine ;
And call me by my name, Lord, for I am Thine ;
Thou wilt stand and wait, I shall so look and SEE,
In the garden of God, I SHALL look up — on THEE.

DOUBLE HYMN.

THE WALK TO EMMAUS.

" He made as though He would have gone further."

I.

'TWAS at this hour, upon the world's great day,
　　Two men of sorrow went upon their way ;
Of bitter death they made their bitter moan,
And One drew nigh, and with them walk'd unknown.

I.

So draw Thou nigh to us, dear and dread Lord ;
So to earth's mourners sacred hope afford ;
If yet we know Thee not, reveal our need,
Show us Thyself, the dead Christ, risen, indeed.

2.

'Twas at this hour the Sacred Wayfarer,
With strange, sweet yearning made their hearts to
　　stir ;
Then when He would go on, as one constrain'd
Of prayer, " Abide with us ;" return'd, remain'd.

2.

So, Lord, abide with us, day is far spent ;
Be Thou constrain'd to this Thy dear intent ;
Hast Thou done all, and shall that all be vain ?
Blest Wayfarer, reveal Thyself again.

3.

'Twas at this hour they won Him to their board,
And suddenly, behold, it was the Lord ! —
For He took bread, and bless'd it, — and anon
He gave it to them. — And the Lord was gone.

3.

So, go not now ; abide, and bless, and break,
'Till all our bread is holy, for Thy sake ;
O Life, be Life indeed, true faith afford,
Let *us* cry, also, " We have seen the Lord."

"*Take, eat.*"

THY body done to death below,
    Thou still dost freely give ;
Thy blood, which is Thy life, bestow,
    And in that life I live.
Jesu, my Lord, I Thee confess,
    Thy love my heaven will be ;
Thy care I crave, Thy name I bless,
    And wish myself with Thee.

Thy glorious gift to me make known,
    O yield it from above ;
Bless me according to Thine own
    And not my feeble love ;
Thou wilt not less than I have sought,
    But more, my Saviour, give,
Albeit Thy promise passeth thought,
    In me to grow to live.

I take and eat ; I bless Thy name,
    Thou mighty to atone ;

6

Live in my heart, and free from blame
   Present it at the throne.
Jesu, my Lord, I Thee confess,
   Thy love my heaven will be ;
Thy care I crave, Thy work I bless,
   And wish myself with Thee.
                     Amen.

" Trust in the Lord alway."

IN the night I think on Thee ;
   I remember me by day
Of Thy care ; but who shall say
To my soul, " It shall not be
   That thou ever fall away " ?

I will trust Thee, who began,
   To go on with might divine,
   This salvation is not mine.
I will trust Thee, lover of man,
   To love on, and prove it Thine.

What if sins I left for dead
   Plead too well again to live,
   (Lord, O hear ; O Lord, forgive,)
How shall I lift up my head,
   Find or peace or palliative ?

There be none, — but Thou wilt stand,
   For Thou art not at the end
   Of Thy mercy, and extend
To me, fall'n, a pitying hand,
   Piercèd hand, Thou sinner's friend.

What if mind and thought decay'd,
  Old, I lose Thee from my ken,
  Thou chiefest of the sons of men,
And Thy worth from memory fade ;
  O ! most loving Lord, what then ?

Nay, but Thou wilt not forget ;
  In Thy memory lives my boast ;
  On the everlasting coast
Thou wilt meet and own me yet,
  To the end and uttermost.

PART OF PSALM LXIV.

EARLY my God I bless ;
    My God, for Thee I long ;
Thy love is all my song,
While through the wilderness,
    A thirsty land, I go,
    Where no sweet waters flow.

Amid distress and strife
    I lift my hands on high,
    Thy name to magnify.
Thy love is better than life ;
    My soul doth hang on Thee,
    Thy right hand holdeth me.

My soul is satisfied,
    E'en as with all good things,
    When she Thy praises sings.
Awake, with Thee doth bide ;
    And sleep beneath the wide
    Shade of Thy sheltering wings.

" To know . . . the fellowship of His sufferings."

O CHRIST of God, in my good days
I found Thee, both in work and praise;
But now the cup of pain I drink
And fail to find Thee there,—and sink.

Sore is the weight doth on me lie,
Jesu, I shall not live but die;
Thee have I loved, yet fear is now,
And though Thou didest, I find not how.

In toil for Thee in holy strife
Thy death was hid from me by life;
Now sinks my heart, now fails my breath,
Thy life is hid from me by death.

I faint, and at Thy Cross lie low;
There is no resting, Lord, but so!
The abhorrèd nails my lips do meet,
My arms embrace Thy bleeding feet.

O depth of pain : forget, my soul,
Thy little part ; behold the whole.
O Christ, Thy thorns have woundèd me,
Of Thee redeem'd, I bleed with Thee.

What dost Thou tell me, dying Lord,
Am not I near to heed Thy word?
I mourn for God, I make my cry
In union with Thy death to die.

My soul drawn nearer sweetness finds ;
The fellowship of suffering binds ;
In this dark hour Thou teachest me
My soul is in the dark — with Thee.

I will lay hold, O death divine,
Till all my will is lost in Thine ;
Till grief a balm in union prove,
And suffering be assuaged with love.

" *He gave thanks.*"

OUR Saviour fear'd the suff'ring that should be,
 The sorrow welling up — a mighty sea,
The shame and passion, the last agony,
 And death's cold blanks ;
But yet He took the bread while they did sup,
And — all His will to God's will given up —
He bless'd it ; then, my soul, He took the cup,
 And He gave thanks.

Ay, He gave thanks ; look'd on His symbols true,
The broken body and shed blood ; He knew —
Wonderful love ! — how near the trial drew
 He must endure.
God's will reveal'd for deepest suffering stood,
He took it, blessing it as very good,
And seal'd it willingly with His best blood
 To make it sure.

Great Gift of God, stand yet in our poor stead,
For Thine own piercèd hands and thorn-crown'd head,

For Thine own body glorious from the dead
  Beyond the banks
Of that cold river ; all, whose cold is o'er,
Give thanks. Stand sweetly on Thy happy shore
And bless this bread ; and for this wine, once more,
  Jesus, give thanks.

Note 2.

"*Cast thy burden upon the Lord.*"

I CAST my cares on Thee,
 Thou wilt not refuse them ;
I cast my cares on Thee,
 Not that I may lose them,
But that Thou may'st take them,
And Thine own cares make them.
  Think, O Lord, on me.

(My babes, my dear distress,
 At Thy feet I leave them ;
I must go — but, bless,
 Saviour, and receive them ;
Nought they heed my weeping,
Take to Thine own keeping,
  My children fatherless.)

I cast my pains on Thee ;
 When I cross the river,
Oh near for love's sake be,
 Thou one comfort giver ;
Pity my sore sighing,
Loose my bands in dying —
  Stand and look on me.

I cast my soul on Thee,
  With her stains and sorrow ;
I, ransom'd, look to see
  A holy, long to-morrow.
Thou that failest never,
I cast all for ever
    On Thy clemency.

Ay, all my cares on Thee,
  Thou wilt not refuse them ;
Ay, all my cares on Thee,
  Not that I may lose them,
But that Thou may'st take them,
And Thine own cares make them.
    Think, O Lord, on me.

" Adam, which was the son of God."

THY son, Adam, was red clay
    Yet ; — but Thou didst see our day ;
All foreknown the ages rise,
And with God is no surprise ;
No-way thwarted was Thy plan
When the serpent tempted man.

Goodness that was never soil'd,
Wisdom that was never foil'd,
Let it now mankind suffice
Once to have been in Paradise,
Seeing, O God, it cannot be
That the serpent conquer'd Thee.

Mourning, sinning, dying, dust,
Holy Slayer, in Thee we trust ;
Thy good children fell — but all
Heaven sang of rising after fall ;
While Thou, Triune God, didst sit
And behold and suffer it.

Otherwhile and otherwhere,
Neighbour countries of despair,
Know man's sighing and the weight
Of his toil outside the gate ;
Drink his blood, cover his head
'Neath their sward when he is dead.

But when time is agèd grown
That great mystery shall be known ; —
At the world's foundation slain
Known the Lamb that lives again,
And the grace He did conceive
When the serpent tempted Eve.

*" There shall in no wise enter into it anything
that defileth."*

O ZION on the sacred hills,
　Fair mystery of mysteries!
The noon of God her presence fills,
　The city of our solemnities.

O shall I up her pathways wend,
　And hear afar the rapt strange hymn,
Where shooting rainbow-lights ascend
　Above the chanting seraphim?

Her golden gates all ills outbar;
　The shining river through her fleets
In palmy shade; and angels are
　The common people of her streets.

I know not how, if unaware
　I met the Christ 'neath some fair tree,
To hear Him speak my soul could bear,
　Nor die of joy and no more be.

But since Thou knowest, who dost afford
　This boon above all other grace,
I trust, even I, to see the Lord,
　And bear the beauty of His face.

"O let not the Lord be angry, and I will pray but this once."

EMPTIED of good, with many cares oppress'd,
   Full oft I long to cast them on Thy breast ;
But not that I may lose them, Love Divine,
O rather craving Thou wouldst count them Thine. ,

They are not cares for my poor wants nor loss ;
Their sorrows — whom I love — are my worse cross :
Do as Thou wilt with me, all shall me please,
Only be gracious, Perfect Love, to these

Whose souls I thus present before Thy Throne.
It is not hard to trust Thee with mine own —
But these — they mourn for griefs, they may not flee,
And I can tell them, Lord, to none but Thee.

O might I pray, " Do Thou as I would do
For those I love — were my love strong as true."
But who may ask Thee thus, though long withstood,
He mourneth after God and after good?

" As I would do." Ah ! now methinks I hear
Thy comforting, kind voice, my Lord, most dear ;
I feel Thy grace, Thy sweetness on me shine —
Poor is my treasure-store of love to Thine.

What wouldst thou have me learn?—my trust, my all;
I call down blessings — grief and trouble fall —
And yet Thy heavenly whisper teacheth me
Love is of God, and mine is born of Thee.

There is but one love, and its will is one;
But Thy love seeth all things — my love none.
Mine eyes are held, for so, and only so,
My love would cast their lot, if I might know.

Then take, Lord, on Thyself my load of care,
Kind to my fear, and gentle with my prayer;
With these it shall be well, my rest is one,
Because Thou lov'st them most — Thy will be done.

Note 3.

THE BROODING OF THE DOVE.

I.

" To-day shalt thou be with Me in Paradise."

THOU, when the dying Jesu bled,
Didst mourn upon Him hard bestead,
And when His Spirit He set free,
In death didst gather it to Thee,
And, folded to Thy hallow'd breast,
Didst bear it to a place of rest,
And show unto all saints that wait
In the country of souls separate.

There didst Thou move them, and they rose
At this great Coming, from repose ;
Look'd on Love's advent, knew Love's claim,
And learn'd at last Love's mighty name ;
While Aaron's priests, of Thee made wise,
Approached th' Eternal sacrifice ;
And seers attain'd by Thee reveal'd
The mystery of their visions seal'd.

7

Behold Him, erst so dimly shown,
One that was wounded of His own ;
Behold Him, stricken for man's need,
The afflicted God, the woman's seed ;
The Angel of the Presence dread
Who spake in dreams at their bed's head ;
The Captain at His watch all night,
The wrestler until morning light.

Day breaks, for now the wrestler stays —
The morning star reveals its rays ;
A blest to-morrow waited long
Through eons dimm'd with evensong.
Among the ransom'd souls at rest
The Spirit of the Christ is blest,
And far and fast the shadow flies,
To-morrow dawns in Paradise.

The dying thief beholds that ray
For him the promised, blest " to-day ;"
Light of all worlds whose earliest sheen
Is given to Hades " the unseen."
Peace, peace, our song shall be of peace ;
O, suffering Love, Thy troubles cease,
The holy dead receive the word,
And rest together with the Lord.

THE BROODING OF THE DOVE.

II.

" Ye shall be baptized with the Holy Ghost."

ASCENDED to His Father's throne,
 The Christ was gone from mortal view:
He left a promise with His own,
 " The Comforter shall come to you."

And opening on His earthward way
 All-hallow'd wings, the brooding Dove
Came down and moved till His great day
 On the deep waters of God's love.

Moved, as with forming wings of yore,
 He moved on voids of man untrod ;
A Seer, beholding long before
 The yet unformèd Church of God.

Then, as a rushing wind come down,
 A holy storm of swift desire,
On humble heads a more than crown,
 He fell in hovering tongues of fire.

In ecstasy of love he came,
   The Dove of God to be their guest ;
And they beheld the sacred flame —
   Their power, their sanction, and their rest.

O fall on us.   Thy life afford ;
   Is not the promise made to all ?
Refining fire, informing Lord,
   Indwelling Spirit, fall — O fall.

"*I am ready to depart.*"

NOW my sun will soon depart;
　　Quiet is the closing day,
God doth gently smooth the way,
　　And with peace my waiting heart
　　　　　Still endow.

Wine of life, 'tis well-nigh spent,
　　Work is over, rest is near;
Let me watch for Thee, nor fear
　　When Thy summons shall be sent,—
　　　　　" Enter thou."

Bridegroom at a feast divine,
　　Earth her best doth first afford,
And the worser afterward;
　　But Thou hast kept the good wine
　　　　　Until now.

" There is a river the streams whereof make glad
the city of our God."

LIKE a great river Thy love flows,
 Let not it run to waste,
I'll dip my hand, so near it goes,
 Sure I thereof may taste.

I'll lay me down upon its brink
 And cry to Thee, " Give, give,
I am athirst ; give me to drink."
 He answers, " Drink, and live ;

" How deep the water, thirsting soul,
 Thou canst not see nor dream ;
All is for all, thou hast the whole
 Of great love's lasting stream.

. " Yea, all is thine, and I am thine,
 Thy thirst, thy longing slake ;
Drink, O belovèd, My divine
 Sorrow and love partake.

" Sorrow, for I have sorrow'd much
  Over thy sins and shame ;
Love, for My love is given to such
  As think upon My name.

" Thee will I clothe in raiment white,
  And give thee a white stone ;
Dear shall thy name be in His sight,
  By whom 'tis read alone.

" Thou shalt have place in this My heart
  And hear My heaven-sweet call ;
Behold Me offer'd, take thy part
  In love's unending all."

I will kneel down, and Thee my whole
  Accept, since Thou art won ;
There is great silence in my soul
  As glory were begun ; —

I will kneel down for my new name,
  To thank Thee and to pray,
" Preserve it, Saviour, free from blame
  Until the judgment day ; " —

I will kneel down, in white robes clad,
  And from its bordering sod,
Drink of the river that makes glad
  The city of my God.

EVENING.

"Man goeth forth to his work and to his labor till the evening."

THE sun is gone, the long clouds break
And sink adown his golden wake ;
Behold us, met now work is done
To seek Thy grace at evensong.

Half-hearted, tardy, cold are we,
Warm us, and draw our souls to Thee ;
Draw us to follow, as the sun,
Thy servant, vassal worlds draws on.

Break to us, dealer of man's bread,
Food fresh from heaven as manna spread,
Lest of the poisonous fruits of death
Eat the sad soul that hungereth.

We would not meagre gifts down-call
When Thou dost yearn to yield us all ;
But for this life, this little hour,
Ask all Thy love and care and power.

Show us Thy pureness, here, on earth ;
Into Thy kingdom give us birth.
We would not wish or dare, to wait
In better worlds a better state.

But save us now, and cleanse us now,
Receive each soul and hear its vow :
" My father's God, on Thee I call,
Thou shalt be my God, and my All."

"*I am the true Vine, and My Father is the
Husbandman.*"

NOW will I sing a song I learn'd of old
    To One whom my soul loveth. " O my Vine,
My Life, Thy branch cries out to Thee ; behold,
    For good, this fruitless graft, that yet is Thine.

Alas, for clusters it should bear to Thee
    Leaves that do languish, wither'd buds are there ;
When the Great Husbandman shall presently
    Come down, is nothing sweet, and nothing fair.

That branch He favour'd of the almond tree
    Budded, brake forth, and bloom'd in Aaron's hand ;
O mystic Vine, shall He do less for Thee
    Than bid Thy favour'd branch revive, expand.

Call the sweet winds of heaven and bid them blow,
    And call the clouds to drop in gracious dew ;
Let Thy sap rise in this dry branch and flow —
    (For yet 'tis Thine) — Rise, rise, in it anew.

O for his Hand, the Heavenly Husbandman ;
　　But what if it should come with loss, with pain ?
How should the wheat desire the winnowing fan —
　　How shall the branch desire so sore a gain ?

Nay, let that be.　Only, my Life, my Vine,
　　Thee let me yet some sweetness grow, and then
It shall suffice Thy branch — (is it not Thine ?) —
　　To ask, to pray, " Even so come.　Amen."

SERVICE.

" Jesus saith unto her, ' Give Me to drink.' "

IT was the heat of afternoon : To Sychar thus befell
That her Messias came to her, and sat by Jacob's
well
Aweary, for the way was long — He lean'd upon the
brink —
Cometh a woman down to draw — "Give Me," saith
He, " to drink."

" And O," cries many a heart to-day, in love and yearn-
ing true,
" So would that I," and " Would that I," and " Would
that I might do ;"
And " Would that in that woman's place it might have
been for me
To draw the water Thou didst long for — Blessèd
One — for Thee."

The well was deep the woman drew, and to His sacred
mouth
Did lift the water, nothing 'ware of ought but mortal's
drouth ;

Then ask — O sad, O sweet her words — of Him,
    blest Son of Man,
" How is it Thou wilt ought of me, th' unloved Samar-
    itan? "

How is it, mighty Love of God, O Great Messias, how!
Thou wilt of sinners ask for aid, thou wilt " have deal-
    ings " now?
"Give Me to drink, the well is deep, I sit, I wait for
    thee ;
I am athirst, I am athirst ; 'beseech you, succour Me !

" For thou and I, and these My poor, are one ; their
    need is Mine,
And whoso aideth mortal want, so aideth My divine."
I yield Thee hearty thanks, O Lord ! So yet, it mine
    may be
To draw the water Thou dost long for — Blessèd One —
    For Thee.

DOUBLE HYMN.

"*Here am I; send* ME."

I.

MY Jesu! In the crowd He walks with sorrow's
       down-trod sons;
He is afflicted in the streets for His afflicted ones.
Lord Jesu, buffeted again while rushing crowds go by,
He pleadeth for His poor unheard, for His oppress'd
    doth sigh.

2.

What are these wounds, Thou Love of God, so low
    that condescends?
Alas! Thou'rt wounded in the house, my Jesu, of Thy
    friends;
I will go down into the streets, for sure Thou beck-
    onest me;
Go down, Thou Saviour of my heart, and serve Thy
    poor with Thee.

I.

Once the fishers Thine appearing
    Saw, and cried for aid;
Want and toil behold Thee nearing
    Now, no more afraid.

Dear to misery's sons and daughters,
  Now Thy visits be,
Walking on the whelming waters
  Of their stormy sea.

3.

My Jesu! On the height He walks a-shepherding
   His sheep ;
A little flock, a scatter'd flock new waken'd out of
   sleep,
For slumber yet their heavy eyes can scarce His
   beauty see,
And " Who will climb upon the heights and tend this
   flock for Me? "

4.

Dear, my Lord Jesu, my desire, the lonely paths are
   high ;
The scatter'd flock doth wander oft, and deep the
   snow-drifts lie ;
But in Thy pleasure is my life, Thy will my law shall
   be ;
Lo ! I will climb upon the heights and tend this flock
   for Thee.

2.

There, one day, O Lord, their only
  Trust, shall sound Thy feet
Coming up the pastures lonely,
  In remoteness sweet.

Coming, in the dim, the golden
    Dawn ere shadows flee
As Thou camest in ages olden —
    Walking on the sea.

5.

My Jesu! walking on the strand, a ship about to sail,
And "All My love to them she bears, is but an un-
    known tale ;
Where is the man will tell My tale and dare the desert
    sea,
Albeit, he take his life in hand, and sailing meet —
    with Me ? "

6.

Lord Jesu, I will sail this night, and tell Thy story o'er,
E'en though unto the land beloved return the ship no
    more,
For O sweet death, and O sweet death, if death my
    dower should be,
Even so come, Lord Jesus, — come, and meet us on
    the sea.

3.

When the rent heavens rage and thunder,
    When the unfriended barque
Beaten of the deep goes under,
    Foundering in the dark ;

When the yeasty waves all cover,
   When the spirits flee —
Meet them, mankind's Lord and lover,
   Walking on the sea.

8

HARVEST.

" Praise the Lord, O my soul."

THOU giv'st to men the fruitful land,
    And harvests from the deep;
By day Thou giv'st with bounteous hand,
    By night Thou giv'st in sleep.
Thou giv'st the wakening of the spring,
    In autumn sheaves to live;
We give but thanks, our God, O King,
    Nought else we have to give.

While I have breath I'll praise the Lord,
    Who doth me hold in life;
Of His own life did me afford,
    And shared my bread, my strife.
By me did toil, and with me housed,
    Consider'd sore my doom;
My misery rued, my cause espoused,
    And made with me His tomb.

He paid my debt, and in three days
    The sting of death He stole ;
Now am I glad, that was full sad
    And sick ;—in Him made whole.
O heaven and earth, high praise afford,
    Thou deep its echoes roll ;
Praise ye the Lord, praise ye the Lord —
    Praise the Lord, O my soul.

CONFLICT.

"Show me wherefore Thou contendest with me."

ART Thou come down my life to end
    In the dark, with Thy dread might?
I am nought: O how should I contend?
And I did think Thou wert my friend,
    Thou Wrestler in the night.

Why is Thy hand so heavy on me? —
    I faint — I am undone;
I fall — there once was pity with Thee;
By Thy past pity, O set me free,
    My Lord, my Holy One.

Thy dust cries to Thee from the ground,
    Lord, Thou hast laid me low;
All my sins rise and hem me round,
In the dark accusing whispers sound —
    I, whither shall I go?

I have dwelt careless ; yet, methought
  Thy smiles on me were sure ;
I have done amiss and evil wrought ;
Now, in great darkness, I am taught
  How, Lord, Thine eyes are pure.

Is Thy great sum of kindness told ?
  Nay, through all tears, I wot
Thou art nearer to me than of old ;
While Thou dost strive I can Thee hold.
  Slay, — but depart Thou not.

Hear me. Thy strokes are not the whole
  These bitter tears deplore.
To have grieved Thy heart is my worse dole ;
Forgive, blest Wrestler, with my soul
  I would Thee wound no more.

Thou art Thyself though Thou dost chide
  My one hope, all my grace ;
O Love ! I cannot be denied ;
O Christ ! Thou wilt not me divide
  From the comfort of Thy face.

Give yet a blessing ere day break.
  I shall not see Thee here,
But I have held Thee ; — do not take
Away Thy hand till Thou me make
  Glad in Thy love and fear.

" Thy gentleness hath made me great."

NOW winter past, the white-thorn bower
    Breaks forth and buds down all the glen ;
Now spreads the leaf and grows the flower :
    So grows the life of God, in men.

Oh, my child-God, most gentle King,
    To me Thy waxing glory show ;
Wake in my heart as wakes the spring,
    Grow as the leaf and lily grow.

I was a child, when Thou a child
    Didst make Thyself again to me ;
And holy, harmless, undefiled,
    Play'd at Thy mother Mary's knee.

Thou gav'st Thy pure example so,
    The copy in my childish breast
Was a child's copy.   I did know
    God, made in childhood manifest.

Now I am grown, and Thou art grown
  The God-man, strong to love, to will,
Who was alone, yet not alone,
  Held in His Father's presence still.

Now do I know Thee for my cure,
  My peace, the Absolver for me set ;
Thy goings pass through deeps obscure,
  But Thou with me art gentle yet.

Long-suffering Lord, to man reveal'd
  As One that e'en the child doth wait,
Thy full salvation is my shield,
  Thy gentleness hath made me great.

" Jesus saith unto them, ' Children, have ye any meat ?' "

A S a pillar on the shore,
    Darkly dim the Christ they see ;
Ere the morning watch is o'er —
" Children, have ye any meat ? "
    He doth ask them tenderly.

" Nay, and we have toil'd all night ;
    Weary casts do nought afford."
In the sudden morning light,
Now they know Him — fearful, sweet
    To their hearts — it is the Lord.

" Children, have ye any meat ? "
    Still of faith He questions thus ;
Lo we, kneeling at His feet,
Answer, " Ay, the meal is spread,
    Bless and break, and give to us."

" Children, have ye any meat ?
    Ought of Mine or ought of Me ? "
" Ay, this living bread to eat ;
Ay, these drops for healing shed ;
    Ay, Lord Jesus, we have Thee."

"Wilt thou be made whole?"

A LL in still heat the waters lie,
 And one doth watch with faded eye;
But never angel wings are sent
To move them, for him impotent.

How long? How long? Lo, One at hand,
Untroubled as the pool doth stand;
In power He meets the suffering soul,
Demanding, " Wilt thou be made whole?"

Wilt thou, so long time in this case?
Strange words but wondrous is the face;
He will, and straight the blessing won,
He riseth, all his dolour done.

" Thy lips are full of grace," O Lord,
Yet Thy words wound as doth a sword;
Not weary watch, nor healing wave,
Nor angel wings, they cry, can save.

Thou showest to man Thy dear intent,
And waitest for his will's consent;
Repeating to the sin-struck soul,
"WILT thou, poor sufferer, be made whole?"

Wilt thou?   Is mighty Love, thy meed
Only to make me whole?   Dost plead
Only to give me all : O still
Help the heart's answer, " Lord, I will."

ADVENT.

" Behold, a king shall reign in righteousness."

THERE was a seer who spake of old,
    " Though God be all my stay;
Zion, thy sons shall yet behold
    A fairer, sweeter day.
In the city of David light shall spring,
    Judgment her gates shall bless;
A Man shall be the peace — a King
    Shall reign in righteousness.

" As a covert from the stormy wind,
    Behold this man shall be;
A sheltering ark they shall Him find
    Upon a rain-vexed sea.
As cold water to a thirsting flock
    Errant on sultry sand,
As the shadow of a great rock
-   In a weary land."

Cast every crown thy kings have worn,
    O earth, before great heaven;

Cry " Unto us the child is born,
  To us the Son is given."
He bringeth peace to men of peace .
  The poor His name confess ;
Behold the Man ! the world's release,
  The Lord, our Righteousness.

"*I will arise.*"

A STILL small voice would fain me rouse :
  " Hungry thou art and lone,
Very far from thy Father's house,
  And no man heeds thy moan."

" Come to thyself, what hast thou got
  But misery for thy pains?
They grudge thee e'en thine evil lot —
  Scant husks and sordid gains.

" Lo, thou art lost, — and peace no more
  About thy path doth shine ;
Thou hast no home, and 'tis thy sore
  To see the blame all thine.

" Thou hast earn'd stripes to rue their smart —
  Wholly thou art undone ;
No pity — none — but in His heart
  Who counts thee yet a son.

"O thou poor soul, why wilt thou die?
    Thy Father's door stands wide;
A great way off He hears thee cry,
    Thou shalt not be denied.

"Answer His love, nor fear rebuff,
    Thy all of hope there lies;
Answer Him, 'Lord, it is enough;
    Father, I will arise.'"

NEW YEAR'S EVE; OR, "THE WATCH-NIGHT."

*"Awake, thou that sleepest, and arise from the dead,
and Christ shall give thee light."*

THOU that sleepest not afraid,
  Men and angels thee upbraid ;
Rise, cry, cry to God aloud,
Ere the swift hours weave thy shroud :
    O, for Jesus' sake,
      Wake !

Thee full ill doth it beseem
Through the dark to drowse and dream ;
In the dead-time of the night
Here is One can give thee light :
    O, for Jesus' sake,
      Wake !

The year passeth — it and all
God shall take and shall let fall
Soon, into the whelming sea
Of His wide eternity :
    O, for Jesus' sake,
      Wake !

Noiseless as the flakes of snow
The last moments falter and go ;
The time-angel sent this way
Sweeps them like a drift away :
    O, for Jesus' sake,
      Wake !

Loved and watch'd of heaven, for whom
The crowned Saviour there makes room,
Sleeper, hark ! He calls thee, rise,
Lift thy head, and raise thine eyes !
    Now, for Jesus' sake,
      Wake !

*" There was a sound as of a mighty rushing wind, and
it filled all the house where they were met."*

HOLY of Holies, forming Mind,
Not as a mighty rushing wind,
Thy great descent we look to greet,
And fill this house wherein we meet.

Not a refining fire to see,
As did Thy saints of Galilee ;
But give the better grace to hold,
Thy coming dear as held of old.

They fasted, waited, pray'd for Thee,
Yet knew not what the gift would be ;
And when Thy mighty presence came,
Amazed they wore the crowning flame.

We know — and seek not — we desire
Nor rushing wind nor falling fire ;
We know, but ask a slender dole,
And lips and life deny the whole.

He giveth to His Church no more
The gifts, she saith, bestow'd of yore ;
But could she dare to fast, to pray
For such a dower in such a day.

A gift once more to set apart, —
And close to her the world's kind heart —
Her world forgiven, her all too dear,
The sister she hath lived so near ?

Yet, let her cry, " What have I done,
I that have lost who might have won ;
Let me no more Thy gifts restrain,
Albeit my heart they rend in twain.

" Give all Thou wilt give !   Anger, scorn,
Yea fire, yea sword, yea lives forlorn
To follow if they must — yet give.
Set us apart, and let us live.

" False friends no more that falsely greet,
'Twere good to part, so best to meet ;
A mighty church made strong to hold
The awaken'd world within her fold."

'

EARLY QUESTIONS OF THE CHURCH.

" Who shall roll us away the stone from the door of the sepulchre ? "

CHURCH of God, these many years
Watching at the door with tears ;
" Christ is risen," Angels said ;
Mourn not, worship not the dead.

For a dead Christ these made moan,
While death held Him had they none,
And would fain have found them room
For their misery in His tomb.

O how gentle to their grief —
Lord, how swift to bring relief ;
Only three days dead, — and now
Living, asks, " Why weepest thou ? "

As to them He died in vain,
Till in life He stood again ;
So till faith His rising see,
Church of God, it is with thee.

Thou art dead, while He is dead ;
Dead to thee.   Behold, thy head.
Life, in Him thy life, He giveth —
Know that thy Redeemer liveth.

Life, Creator, Son, all fair,
By Whose power the worlds first were,
By Whose rule the heavens were laid,
In Whose likeness man was made.

Word, with speech, that made man wise,
Lord, that walk'd in Paradise —
Over vague leagues, pale with light,
Steer'd the sailing ark aright —

Forty years abode with Shem
In his tents, and marshall'd them —
Show'd to seers unearthly things —
Visited the dreams of kings —

Bearing, yearning, reigning, kind,
Taught to man Thy righteous mind —
In the dark world gone astray,
Wakening hope of some good day —

Saviour — what we lost who won,
And much more for us undone ;
Thou hast been since time began
Only three days dead to man.

Diedst Thou then that we should sleep?
Didst Thou rise that we should weep?
Church of God, rise thou — and shine;
Sing for joy, "Thy life is mine."

In His death forgiveness lies,
By His rising thou dost rise;
Day by day thy life He giveth,
Sing, for thy Redeemer liveth.

" Though I walk through the valley of the shadow of
death I will fear no evil."

TELL to us, tell, O Church of God,
    Where is thy faithful Shepherd gone ?
Green pastures of His foot untrod ;
    Still waters all unsmiled upon.

" My Shepherd is a great King's heir,
    With whom He bides in bliss untold,
And for His flock makes ready there,
    The safe, the everlasting fold.

" Thence doth He watch whom He did choose ;
    He counts the flock, and knoweth them all ;
His sheep and lambs He will not lose,
    And one by one He doth them call.

" There is a valley they must tread,
    Where lieth the shadow of a sleep,
Dark is the shadow ; but they dread
    No evil, He their steps will keep.

" It is the great way home to Him,
    The golden gates He entered so.
Hark, hark ! I hear in darkness dim
    The songs of them that down it go.

" Thou, O good Shepherd, art my stay,
    I will not fear the gloom to see,
For death, since Thou hast pass'd this way,
    Is but the shadow of death to me."

EASTER.

"Blessed be the Lord for evermore.   Amen, and Amen."

IN the valleys of Immanuel's land,
   Are there high-days, holier than the rest?
One another, with salutings bland,
   Greet the saints upon the birthday blest?
In Immanuel's land, so far away,
If they keep e'en now their Easter day
Alleluias, none can reach our ken;
Yet, earth, make sweet thine answer — " Amen."

There, it may be sometime from His throne
   Coming down, Immanuel walks the shade;
Saints beneath the palm-trees, one by one,
   Hear a man's sweet voice, no whit afraid,
Making mention of His sojourn here;
Then all angels sing in joyance clear
Alleluias.   O they pass our ken;
Yet, earth, make sweet thine answer — " Amen."

Sweetly now Immanuel's voice may sound,
   "As upon this day in Salem old,
Me My sorrowing mother, Mary, found
   'Mid the Father's courts of beaten gold ;
When a child I knew not all My part,
And desired it of My Father's heart."
Alleluias sang the angels then ;
O, earth, make sweet thine answer — "Amen."

Or, it may be He is heard to speak
   While the winds of heaven about Him blow,
Looking down from some high, glorious peak
   On the far-off earth that spins below ;
"There, as on this day my work all o'er,
I slept to God and woke to sleep no more ; "
Alleluias sang the angels then.
O, earth, make sweet thine answer — "Amen."

"Thou thoughtest that I was altogether such an one
as thyself."

WOULD I, to save my dear child dutiful,
   Dare the white breakers on a storm-rent
     shore ?
Ay, truly, Thou all good, all beautiful,
   Truly I would, — then truly Thou would'st more.

Would I for my poor son, who desolate
   After long sinning, sued without my door
For pardon, open it ? Ay, fortunate
   To hear such prayer, I would, — Lord, Thou would'st
     more.

Would I for e'en the stranger's weariness
   And want divide, albeit 'twere scant, my store?
Ay, and mine enemy, sick, shelterless,
   Dying, I would attend, — O, Lord, Thou more.

In dust and ashes my long infamy
   Of unbelief I rue.   My love before
Thy love I set : my heart's discovery,
   Is sweet, — whate'er I would, Thou wouldest more.

I was Thy shelterless, sick enemy,
   And Thou didst die for me, yet heretofore
I have fear'd ; now learn I love's supremacy, —
   Whate'er is known of love, Thou lovest more.

"*Why stand ye gazing.*"

WAS never sight so wondrous given?
  Yet angels talk with them that see;
"Why stand ye gazing up to heaven,"
  They ask, "ye men of Galilee?"

"What should we do, but ever gaze?
  The earth is void, the heavens are cleft
Of Him gone up the steep highways
  To God,—this hour are we bereft.

"Lo, love cries upward, hope is cross'd,
  We, following glad through tears would fall,
E'en rapt with our sweet listening lost, —
  The blessèd One, the all in all.

"Once from our boats He taught, He trod,
  Alas, unknown, the field, the shore;
To-day He was our present God,
  And we shall see His face no more.

"Why, O ye white ones, question thus?
  The Christ for heaven bereaves His own,
And what is left on earth for us
  But still to gaze where He is gone?"

The angels answer. "Lo," they say,
  While steadfast eyes those watchers strain,
"This Jesus, caught to heaven to-day,
  Shall in like manner come again."

"His feet on Olivet shall stand;
  Ay, this same Jesus shall come down."—
Spare Him, O God, from Thy right hand,
  Most holy Saviour, take Thy crown.

Son of the Father, hear: our night
  Is dark, Thy mourners wait and yearn.
O Lamb of God, O Light of Light,
  O Love of Love, return, return!

"*He first loved us.*"

I SOUGHT the Lord, and afterward I knew
   He moved my soul to it Who sought for me ;
It was not I that found, O Saviour true ;
    No, I was found of Thee.

Thou didst reach forth Thy hand and mine enfold ;
   I walk'd and sank not on the storm-vexed sea ;
But not so much that I on Thee took hold
    As by Thy hold of me.

I find, I walk, I love, but ah, the whole
   Of love is but my answer, Lord, to Thee ;
Lord, Thou wert long beforehand with my soul —
    Always Thou lovèdst me.

" Where two or three are met together, there am I in the midst of you."

THE meaning of Thy meat and drink,
    Lord, is for me too high ;
And so much more than I can think,
    As Thou art more than I.

But for remembrance, and for hope,
    In faith that cannot see,
I, raised above life's narrow scope,
    Reach forth my prayer for Thee.

Bless me, and for Thy blessèd sake,
    From love's un'minish'd store
Whatever I have learn'd to take,
    Lord Jesus, give me more.

I come to meet Thee, Thou art here,
    Standing among Thine own ;
For "two or three" that hold Thee dear
    Have drawn Thee, Saviour, down.

I come, my nothing I confess,
    Thy all I cannot know ;
But till Thou to the utmost bless
    I will not let Thee go.

THE EARLY QUESTIONS OF THE CHURCH.

"Art Thou He that should come?"

JESUS, the Lamb of God, gone forth to heal and
    bless.
Calm lie the desert pools in a fair wilderness ;
Wind-shaken moves the reed, so moves His voice the
    soul ;
Sick folk surprised of joy, wax when they hear it,
    whole.

Calm all His mastering might, calm smiles the desert
    waste ;
Peace, peace, He shall not cry, nay, He shall not
    make haste ;
Heaven gazes, hell beneath moved for Him, moans
    and stirs —
Lo, John lies fast in prison, sick for his messengers.

John, the forerunner, John, the desert's tameless son,
Cast into loathèd thrall, his use and mission done ;
John from his darkness sends a cry, but not a plea ;
Not, "Hast Thou felt my need?" but only, "Art Thou
    He?"

Unspoken pines his hope, grown weak in lingering
    dole ;
None know what pang that hour might pierce the
    Healer's soul ;
Silence that faints to Him — but must e'en so be vain ;
A word — the fetters fall — He will that word restrain.

Jesus, the Father's son, bound in a mighty plan,
Retired full oft in God, show'd not His mind to
    man ;
Nor their great matters high His human lips confess ;
He will His wonders work, and not make plain, but
    bless.

The bournes of His wide way kept secret from all
    thought,
Enring'd the outmost waste that evil power had
    wrought ;
His measure none can take, His strife we are not
    shown,
Nor if He gather'd then more sheaves than earth hath
    grown.

"John, from the Christ of God, an answer for all
    time,"
The proof of Sonship given in characters sublime ;
Sad hope will He make firm, and fainting faith re-
    store,
But yet with mortal eyes will see His face no more.

He bow'd His sacred head to exigence austere,
Unknown to us and dark, first piercings of the spear:
And to each martyr since 'tis even as if He said,
" Verily I am He — I live, and I was dead.

" The All-wise found a way — a dark way — dread,
     unknown ;
I chose it, will'd it Mine, seal'd for My feet alone ;
Thou canst not therein walk, yet thou hast part in
     Me,
I will not break thy bonds, but I am bound with thee.

"With thee and for thee bound, with thee and for
     thee given,
A mystery seal'd from hell, and wonder'd at in heaven ;
I send thee rest at heart to love, and still believe ;
But not for thee — nor Me — is found from death
     reprieve."

THE MILKY WAY.

" Verily Thou art a God that hidest Thyself, O God of Israel, the Saviour."

THE summer night draws near its noon ;
   The wheat fields rustle nigh ;
A golden reaping-hook — the moon
   Hangs like a sign on high.

As if to mind us of His care,
   Who guides the worlds o'erhead,
Yet gives us in His heart a share,
   And thinks upon our bread.

Sign to them sent, whose marvelling eyes
   Pierce to thought's outmost bars,
Where faint, because of farness, lies
   Light, as the dust of stars.

My dazzled thoughts toward it strain,
   Where bedded deep in space,
All twisted like a house-wife's skein
   The myriads interlace ;

Wonderful suns! a nameless mote,
  No more, is each to me;
Wonderful worlds that round them float,
  Led forth, great God, of Thee.

They strew Thy road as golden sand;
  How far, to think we fear,
For all within Thy presence stand,
  And we, as they, are near.

Thou didst not tell to men of old
  How great Thy goings were;
Hiding Thy power, Thou didst unfold,
  Father revered, Thy care.

Only to us, Thy wonders wrought
  (Like some of those far rays)
Have reach'd, at last, man's watchful thought,
  To light these latter days.

What Thou dost tell in stars above,
  What give we are not shown;
Thou givest all to us — for love
  Is all, and love made known.

So many worlds, Thou central Sun,
  And all Thy brightness here?
It may be not, for only one,
  Thy love has cost Thee dear.

Perhaps full many a starry gem
　Lapsed from Thy grace did lie;
Perhaps, made manifest in them,
　Thy Love went forth to die.

We dwell as at creation's brink,
　Yet saved, and safe from thrall;
We think, if we may dare to think,
　Thou givest all to all.

"*He dwelleth* WITH *you and shall be* IN *you.*"

MIGHTY and merciful, to Thee
   A wearied spirit yearns,
That fain as sacred fire would be,
   Which ever mounts and burns.

Mine eyes attend till night shall flee,
   And come day's golden rim ;
As in Thy shrine of old — with me
   The lamp of God burns dim.

I dwell as, in the days of yore,
   They dwelt, who loved and fear'd,
When Christ within the fasten'd door
   Appear'd and disappear'd :

I dwell as they who blest their day,
   When Christ made void the tomb,
Between a glory going away —
   A glory yet to come :

At rest in hope of sins forgiven
  I walk, His follower true ;
But O to share on this side heaven,
  That promised glory too.

For all Christ died, and once for all,
  No souls in Him are lost ;
But 'tis for each the flame must fall,
  The dower at Pentecost.

My breaking heart for this good hour
  The very heavens would stir ;
He is not come, with Whom is power,
  The Lord, the Comforter.

Rise, wind of God ! Burn, sacred flame !
  This stammering tongue set free ;
And over sins, and sloth, and shame,
  Give Thine own victory.

" The dove found no rest for the sole of her foot."

LORD, how Thou lovest! with each one,
　　Yes, every soul Thou bringest in ;
'Tis as Thou hadst but one alone,
　　So fain Thou art that one to win.

And there is joy reflecting Thine,
　　E'en joy on earth when dangers pass'd ;
Obedience crowns the call divine,
　　That draws Thy wanderers home at last.

Not the tired dove (when he did fold
　　The covering back, and wish for her)
Was to Thy mariner-saint of old
　　At her alighting welcomer —

O not so welcome ! though of Thee
　　Reveal'd, He knew forlorn of shore
She was a type of all should flee
　　To mercy's arms for evermore.

Thou, from the windows cf that ark,
    Which floats upon Thy love's wide sea,
Their trembling, wearied wings dost mark,
    O Lord, who fainting fly to Thee;

Dost take them in, and on Thy breast
    Comfort, and 'neath Thy rule make great;
So, one with Thee, and many that rest
    Safe there to God's name dedicate:

All sailing to the golden wall,
    And serving each in his degree,
For they are all one — even all,
    Bound in the bundle of life with Thee.

That life which warms Thy sacred heart
    Thy one, Thy all (Thou sayest it) share;
O let me in their life have part,
    And love Whose easy yoke they wear.

Put forth Thy hand, take in my soul,
    That in the ark full fain would be;
Live to the whole, and in the whole,
    And of the whole, Thy Church and Thee.

" In my flesh I shall see God."

ALL in the city, whose gates are gold,
  The saints walk softly, unshod,
And gather with Christ from the tree of life,
  And drink of the river of God.

I SHALL SEE HIM, my Lord, all-fair,
  Even I, in the happy land ;
I shall kiss the hem of His raiment there,
  And it may be, touch His hand.

He is my God, and He is a Man
  And His lips do move in speech ;
No words so holy since time began !
  But we know not what they teach :

Save that a Man of Sorrow no more,
  He talketh of bliss unknown,
Till the heavens do laugh to their outmost shore,
  And answers come from the throne.

We shall draw near Him, while none do let,
  Nor any our access blame ;
When close at His feet the saved are met,
  He will know us all by name.

*" O wretched man that I am ! who shall deliver me
from the body of this death ?"*

THOU, who didst bear man's grief of old,
Receive my heart-sick cry ;
O my great Father, I am bold
To speak, let me not die.

Pity Thyself in pity of me,
For Thou dost feel my moan,
Assuage my grief, it paineth Thee :
Lord, it is even Thine own.[1]

Thy spirit in my spirit pleads,
And yearns to ways upright,
With earnest mourning intercedes,
And moves toward the light.

Would I might work Thy perfect will ;
But sin doth yet endure ;
And Thou continuest holy still,
I know that Thou art pure.

[1] In all their affliction He was afflicted.

Father, I hate myself, — but Thou
    Canst love my ruin'd race,
And fain didst spare heaven's rightful heir
    To win us to His place.

My soul admires at His great love,
    His travail sore to fill
With ransom'd men the courts above.
    O let Him have His will.

Let not ought rob Thine only Son,
    Nor foil Thy great decree.
Father of mercies, all is done —
    Well done, and perfectly.

Fain would I walk as He did walk,
    In ways sincere and sure,
Holy in mind, in deed, in talk
    Made pure, as He is pure.

Content Him, save and set me free,
    His wounds are not made whole,
Till in high heaven Thou let Him see
    Of the travail of His soul.

PALM SUNDAY.

"And ye shall take you on the first day, the boughs of goodly trees, branches of palm trees."

AS on this day in the times of yore,
    A King forth fared to His wond'rous ride ;
And a multitude that went before,
    And a multitude that follow'd cried,
                " Hosanna."

They spread their garments beneath His feet,
    And straw'd green palms on the rock-hewn way;
"Great Son of David," in greeting sweet,
    " Blessèd art Thou," they did sing and say ;
                " Hosanna."

Lo, when He mark'd from the mount's descent
    Beautiful Salem in all her pride,
Under the olives He weeping went,
    While bearing their palms her children cried,
                " Hosanna."

Mourner and Monarch, Thy tears are dry ;
    But the song of the palms shall ne'er be o'er,
For the multitudes yet following cry,
    As the multitude gone on before,
                " Hosanna."

THE SAVIOUR'S MESSAGE TO THE ISLANDS CONCERNING ISRAEL.

Isaiah xlix. to ver. 23, and lx. 9.

"Listen, O isles, unto Me."

LISTEN, O Isles, unto Me,
   And hearken ye people from far,
I was hid in the hand of My God,
   I was sent with the light of a star;
I was shown unto Israel, His choice,
   But they would not their Light I should be;
Then I said, "I have labour'd in vain;"
   Yet, surely, My work is with Thee.
   Listen, O Isles, unto Me.

And He said, yea, My Holy One said,
   "Should'st Thou serve Me for Israel alone?
Nay, truly it is a light thing,
   Thou, only begotten, My Son,
To the ends of the earth Thou shalt save,
   Thou shalt reign in the realm of the sea:
For a light to the Gentiles, O Son,"
   Saith My God, "I will ALSO give THEE."
   Listen, O Isles, unto Me.

" I have heard Thee," My Holy One said,
  " I will give Thee for worship and peace,
To light the dark world with Thy love,
  To yield to Thy prisoners release ;
Thou shalt guide where the watersprings flow,
  And wash them, and let them go free ;
Their hunger and thirst Thou shalt bless,
  Who hunger and thirst after Thee."
Listen, O Isles, unto Me.

Sing, O heavens, and be joyful, O earth ;
  But Zion with dust on her head,
" My God hath forgotten me," mourn'd,
  " My Lord hath forsaken me," said.
O Zion, and can I forget ?
  For ever engraven shall be
Thy name on the palms of My hands,
  It was graven anew there of Thee.
Listen, O Isles, unto Me.

Be ready, O Isles, for My day,
  The ships of the Islands shall wait,
My sons and my daughters to bear
  To the land that of old I made great ;
I will bless them, the Isles, I have said,
  " Yea, blessèd, O Israel, shall be,
Who for sake of My name and My love,
  And My life, and My death blesseth Thee."
Listen, O Isles, unto Me.

" Your gold and silver is cankered."

IN foul and cheerless places
   I sought my realm's disgraces ;
The poor — I mark'd their faces — ill they sped ;
   Hard by the forges burning,
   And by the great wheels turning,
Behold them, grimly earning — their bread.

They toil'd amid the fire,
   The deep mines, and the mire,
And won not their desire — nay, nor ease :
   But trouble to them cleavèd
   Till old age unreprievèd,
These have we bereavèd —yea, these.

But as I turn'd me, sighing,
   From their long strife, and crying,
Where my sweet home was lying — fair to see,
   A voice mine ears receivèd,
   The words of One that grievèd,
" ME have ye bereavèd — yea, ME."

" Break, heart, thy brother weepeth ;
And One the record keepeth,
While yet the judgment sleepeth — heed and wake;
His want thy glory fretteth,
His shame thine honour letteth,
Lest God thy name forgetteth — break, break.

" For these, my brethren, pleading
I lie, down-trod and bleeding,
And ye, my wounds unheeding, pass me by ;
Till having lived in pleasure,
In quiet and long leisure,
And heaping up of treasure — ye die.

" Your gold and silver rusteth,
And whoso in them trusteth,
His own soul forth he thrusteth — heaven to flee ;"
The words of One that grievèd, —
" O ye souls deceivèd,
ME have ye bereavèd — yea, ME."

(HYMN WITH A BURDEN.)

" O love the Lord."

AN Island to the Lord of Hosts : —
    " Thou, only Guardian of my coasts,
In Thee the Island nation boasts."
        (O love the Lord.)
" My fields Thou hast not shown a foe,
The noise of battle nor its woe,
Nor smoke of war my children know.
        (I love the Lord.) "

An Island to her King divine : —
" Good is Thy reign o'er me and mine,
Still from Thy throne upon me shine."
        (O love the Lord.)
" To bless with blessings give not o'er,
I have much peace, yet ask for more, —
Give peace at home from shore to shore."
        (O love the Lord.)

"Mould Thou men's hearts to meet their creed,
To righteous walking, Lord, them lead,
And mercy to all souls that need." —
　　　(O love the Lord.)
"To dealings just, a perfect weight,
And in their homes and in their state
To gentleness that maketh great."
　　　(O love the Lord.)

"Yea, Thine for ever be the praise;
Thou wak'nest in these latter days
More longing for Thy perfect ways;" —
　　　(I love the Lord.)
"Morning by morning Thou dost hear
The sighing of Thy children dear,
'Thy will be done,' that will make clear."
　　　(O love the Lord.)

"All-hallow'd soon be Thy great name,
Of such as yet in sinful shame
Lie to their sorrow and our blame."
　　　(O love the Lord.)
"Wake, thou that sleepest! sing, ye dumb,
His goodness is an untold sum;
Wake, wake, and cry, 'Thy kingdom come.'"
　　　(O love the Lord.)

"Look, Lord, on this dear Island still,
And if it stand in Thy blest will,
The prayers of all her saints fulfil."
    (O love the Lord.)
"Yea, though her peace depart away,
Her glory sink as sets the day,
O teach her in her woe to say, —
    (I love the Lord.)"

A REQUIEM.

" I shall go to him, but he shall not return to me."

A WORD to the Greatness on high,
 Sustainer and source of our breath ;
A word from the nations that lie
 Under the shadow of death.

Thou didst show Thee a Father of yore ;
 Father, we bring Thee our dead —
See Thou to the rest evermore,
 Our love's last and utmost is said.

Thou didst show Thee a Saviour divine,
 To ransom from death and from doom ;
Behold now, this dead, he is Thine,
 Laid low at the door of Thy tomb.

Thou didst show Thee a Spirit of Life ;
 Spirit ! O look to Thine own ;
Dust is for dust, — in the strife
 Death conquer'd, heart fail'd, light is gone.

The clod shall lie over — the leaf
　　Shall sparkle in dew o'er his head ;
He is cold, he is deaf to our grief ;
　　He is hid.　O our dead !　O our dead !

Yet, still, Thou great source of our breath,
　　We trust, to the utmost and end ;
O death — the last enemy — death,
　　The dying hath Life for his friend.

When Christ, our true Life, shall appear,
　　The shadow of death forth shall flee,
Thou Life, ever blest, ever dear,
　　We have trusted our dead unto Thee.

*"For Thy name's sake, O Lord, pardon mine iniquity,
for it is great."*

I N great London as I walk'd, and day was dying,
　And a shifting throng unended lined the street,
O, my heart it fell a sighing, fell a sighing,
　For their want, their burden'd lives, their aching
　　feet.

Passing on for whom Christ died, for whom He liveth,
　Whom He pleadeth with and for from age to age;
Trifler, mourner, outcast, erring, though he giveth
　Thought nor care to his great hope and heritage.

O Thy patience, mighty father! Dost Thou show it
　Most to them, or most to us that on Thee call?
Saying, "Lord, we seek Thy way, and yearn to know
　　it;"
　While these others whom Thou lovest want for all.

Want the light and air where, dank, all foulness
　　dwelleth,
　Want the fellowship of saints their hands to take,
Crying, "One are we in Him whose love excelleth;
　Mine is thine, and I am thine for Christ His sake."

I that pray, O turn to labour all the praying;
  I that know Thee, let me know that I may do;
Live to them for whom Thou diedst, neither weighing
  Life nor death, for death shall live, but days are
    few.

So my prayer shall rise unshamed to Thy pure dwell-
    ing,
  While the child of shame low kneeleth me beside.
With Thy other sinful children, while I'm telling
  Thee my sins, I'll pray Thee thus nor go denied.

" Some love darkness more than light, and choose it
    rather;
  Shine and turn them to Thy light, and they shall
    see.
Bear the burdens of the poor, O tender Father,
  Ease the hearts that want, nor know their want is
    Thee.

" My afflicted God, to these afflicted yearning
  Liest Thou low? then bring me low to meet Thee
    there;
Give me, Christ, Thy poor to teach, that with them
    learning
  I may reach Thy feet and hold them, Thou All-Fair.

"O, to these give hope in life and peace in dying;
  Thou hast tasted death, Thou knowest all its stings;
O on me bestow my heart's desire, and sighing
  Still to shepherd them for Thee, Thou Shepherd
    King."

HYMN FOR EDINBURGH.

" The Lord is my light and my salvation."

" BEAUTIFUL for situation,"
    Favour'd in a favour'd nation,
Is she, set in regal station —
    Britain's northern crown.
God has many saints that cry in
Her, — as doves that upward fly in
Heaven's high dome, their prayers they sigh, in
    Edinburgh town.

Prayer He casteth not behind Him ;
No, but they that seek shall find Him,
And with cords of love shall bind Him,
    Sweetly to come down.
Give repentance, Lord, and power,
Double her desires and dower ;
Bless, O bless in this good hour,
    Edinburgh town.

Dry her tears of holy weeping
Over souls in danger sleeping,
And receive her to Thy keeping,
    Great in old renown.
God, make all her goings fair, for
Thy name's sake.   Her, ever care for.
God of nations, hear my prayer for
    Edinburgh town.

ASCENSION DAY.

"He was parted from them, and carried up into heaven."

THOU art gone up, a throne to share,
　Yet doth Thy man's heart, even there,
Partaker of man's yearning care,
　　Love to the end.
The odours of Thine incense fill
The Temple courts, the heavenly hill,
Offer'd with prayers of saints that still
　　Thither ascend.

In love's sweet suffering Thou dost stand,
Touch'd for their tears, Thy pilgrim band,
Who all their griefs in this dark land
　　To Thee commend ;
And mourn, nor think their heavenward quest
Answers the yearning of Thy breast,
Till they to Thee, Who art their rest,
　　Thither ascend.

Blest Lamb of God, for sinners slain,
Wounded Thou art full oft again,
For such as fruitless still remain,
     Or wanderers wend ;
Or like another Eve, the tree
Forbidden, aye desiring see,
Nor heart and mind in heaven — to Thee,
     Thither ascend.

Spare *us* this sin, this evil part,
To wound again Thy sacred heart ;
But still to draw us where Thou art,
     Priest, Saviour, Friend,
Make bright Thy stars —Thy churches seven
Full fill with Thy celestial leaven,
Till all the saints with hearts in heaven
     Thither ascend.

" Unto Thee, O Lord, do I lift up my soul."

THEE my soul desires,
    Thee my heart admires,
Crown'd Messiah, slain ere sin began ;
    All my ways confess Thee,
    And my mouth shall bless Thee,
Mighty son of Mary — God with man.

    Once a soul unheeding,
    Pass'd Thee, Jesus, bleeding ;
I was that poor soul.   Thou pitiedst me.
    Now, Thy mourner, weeping,
    Vow'd to Thy blest keeping ;
I am Thy poor friend that loveth Thee.

    If my short day waneth,
    Lord, Thy light remaineth ;
I shall see it though my sun decline ;
    Sun of my salvation,
    Star of consolation,
Bright and morning Star, arise and shine.

Thee my soul desires,
Thee my heart admires,
Crown'd Messiah, slain ere sin began ;
All my ways confess Thee,
And my heart shall bless Thee,
Mighty Son of Mary — God with man.

" They went forth to meet the Bridegroom."

THAT precious oil we bought of Thee,
    O Bridegroom, watch'd for in the night,
Let not its use and spending be
    Only to keep our lamps alight,

That we by Thee a place may win.
    No, grant us still some light to shed,
Lord, when Thy feet are entering in,
    On the dark dust where Thou wilt tread.

And while Thou tarriest let us take
    Their shining for our joy — Thy grace
To burn and burn, for pure love's sake,
    Spent with aspirings for Thy face.

Look, Father, down from Thy steep heights,
    Speak gently on the great white throne,
"I bless their moving cresset lights,
    Who watch afar for My dear Son."

Lean over from the golden wall,
    O Christ, of all our hopes the sum,
And list, so piercing sweet the call,
    "Thy kingdom come, Thy kingdom come."

" And He said unto him, What is thy name ? and he said, Jacob."

WHILE his God, th' Almighty Lord,
　　Jacob cried on, by the ford,
In a moonless midnight dim ;
Suddenly took hold on him
A greatness, that he could not scan,
A Majesty that was a man.

Now was he in evil case,
His sins look'd him in the face ;
All his soul was dark with fear
Of God's silentness austere ;
Strife till dawn — and cometh then,
Esau, with four hundred men.

Esau, to avenge his wrong,
" O, the blessing trusted long ;
For its cause I, banish'd, bann'd,
Sojourn'd in an alien land ;
Now I feel Thy frown divine,
That teacheth me, it is not mine."

With the Wrestler striving sore,
Still he cries on God the more,
" Wilt Thou — wilt Thou me forgive ? "
But none answering bids him live,
How shall he his cause make good,
One of God and man withstood.

How ! — O Wrestler, hid from sight,
Only yet reveal'd by night,
If thy nature learn'd at length
He took hold upon thy strength,
Thou, and none but Thou, canst know
Who said sweetly, " Let me go."

Nay, no other help is nigh,
If he fail he can but die ;
Turn'd to mourning, and to woe,
Is the birthright bought below ;
For the blessing falsely won,
He, at dawn, shall be undone.

" Wherefore comest Thou then by night,
Ere Thy time ?   Thyself Thy might
To me yielding — till that fail,
Wrestler, how should'st Thou prevail ?
Till Thou me forgiveness show,
I will never let Thee go.

"I confess to Thee my name,
All its meaning, all its blame;
From its misery set me free,
And, departing, bless THOU me,
For on whom Thy blessings rest,
He, I wot, indeed is blest."

So He bless'd him there — and day
Dawn'd, — the Wrestler went His way.
Night to noon, and noon to night,
Still He yields mankind His might;
Wrestling Love He wills to fail,
O my soul, thou shalt prevail!

Note 4.

"*He doeth all things well.*"

THOU hast been alway good to me and mine
    Since our first father by transgression fell.
Through all Thy sorest judgments love doth shine —
    Lord, of a truth, Thou doest all things well.

Thou didst the food of immortality
    Compass with flame, lest he thereto should win.
But what? his doom, yet eating of that tree,
    Had been immortal life of shame and sin !

I would not last immortal in such wise ;
    Desirèd death, not life, is now my song.
Through death shall I go back to Paradise,
    And sin no more — Sweet death, tarry not long !

One did prevail that closèd gate to unseal,
    Where yet th' immortalizing tree doth grow ;
He shall there meet us, and once more reveal
    The fruit of life, where crime is not, nor woe.

*"Righteous art Thou, O Lord, when I plead with Thee,
yet let me talk with Thee of Thy judgments."*

" DARK is my place and chill the night,
    No fire have I, nor candlelight ;
Come down, make good to me Thy word,
O humble and right piteous Lord.
Like to a shadow my days are gone,
Me in this dimness shine upon,
Bring back the shadow in my sight, —
Let there be light, let there be light.

" Righteous art Thou — and I am poor,
And know not good, but long endure ;
I charge it not on Thee, blest Lord,
Enough for all Thy fields afford ;
But some have much and other none,
The weak are robb'd, the mean undone,
And Thou abidest holy and strong, —
O Lord, how long? O Lord, how long?

"There be who care not for Thy grace,
And hide them from Thy frowning face;
If they oppress, O Lord, forgive;
But what of them that in Thee live?
Oft pray Thy rich for us, yet hold
The mastery and increase with gold,
And we, as roots dried up past date,
Lie desolate, lie desolate.

"Righteous art Thou; and they are Thine,
They counsel us in words divine;
But there is no meat and no meal,
And scant is work, and far is weal.
Wandering I go of hunger led,
Hither and thither seeking bread;
Ay, tossing like the salt sea foam,
Till I go home, till I go home.

"Come down and sup with Thy poor friend
That is sore troubled; to me lend
A little comfort.   Nay, good Lord,
Be not displeased — put up Thy sword;
It shall be as Thou wilt with me,
Only Thy goodness let me see;
Shine out and show in sweet advance,
Thy countenance, Thy countenance."

" Peace, thou poor soul, thy Lord is nigh —
Judge not My rich, I judge, even I ;
Pray, rather, pray for them, and weep,
For trouble cometh and shall not sleep ;
But I have chosen the poor to make
Heirs of My God, for Mine own sake ;
Ay, thou hast all ! (O well is thee !)
For thou hast Me, for thou hast Me."

PRAYER AGAINST THE GREAT SEPARATION.

" O that Ishmael might live before Thee."

WHEN I from all I love apart
    Am offering up my chasten'd heart ;
To Thee, O Lord, I make my moan,
Save not, O save not me alone.

Lord God, in misery for my whole,
How am I saved, if I am sole,
My very self, my children dear,
Without a part in Thy sweet fear.

Yea, my most loved ; — yet Thou art love —
Hear me, I come Thy heart to prove,
With long desire and waiting faint,
Opening my grief and my complaint.

Where art Thou, Lord? I cannot rest
Till mine with me are wholly blest ;
My need is now, my prayer is now —
Where art Thou, Lord, why tarriest Thou?

I ask but for a promised good ;
Is't for my sins I am withstood ?
Search me, O God ; behold, and see
If ought of evil cleave to me.

'Tis even so — it must be so,
Yet will I ne'er my hope forego ;
Nay, but I'll rise to regions higher,
Fulfil, O Christ, Thine own desire —

And His that sent Thee.   Let Him rest
Satiate with peace upon Thy breast ;
Let the souls enter, many, and live —
Great Father ; — give to Him — O give.

Yes, when I sink Thou makest me 'ware
They are not left to my poor prayer ;
I move Thee to Thine own intent
To bring these souls from banishment.

O Lord, My God, let it be soon,
My sun declineth from its noon ;
But what ! I know they shall be blest,
I'll dare with Thee to leave the rest.

Although the valley clods be spread
First over mine uncrownèd head,
I know salvation they shall see,
I trust my best-beloved with Thee.

PRAYER AGAINST THE GREAT SEPARATION.

" God is love."

SINCE in Thy likeness man was made,
Love perfect, changeless, undecay'd,
Man's heart looks upward to Thy throne,
His part in Thee desires its own.

I walk in darkness, in the night ;
Thou only, Thou canst give me light ;
The soul of love doth on Thee call,
Who art love's source, its end, its all.

Master of love, O pity me !
Whose love is what I have of Thee ;
Shall one come in — one ever left,
Divided, darken'd, lost, bereft ?

Could I forget ?   Thine own heart knows,
Love is remembrance, and love grows.
Wilt Thou but one Thy life afford ?
O, that be far from Thee, Good Lord.

Could I forget, albeit on high?
Nay; but I'll trust Thee. Heed my cry,
Thou wondrous God, who once did know
For Love's best sake, Love's deepest woe.

Who once for thirty years and three
(Love sent from heaven) sustainedst Thee
Apart, and knew as seem'd Thee good,
Mysterious, awful solitude.

By that dread parting I implore;
By that great meeting, more, Lord, more;
Thou triune God upon the throne,
Remember such as pray alone.

Remember why Thou didst so part
With the great Son of Thy great heart,
And not for ever, Lord, decree
Division betwixt mine and me.

O Lord of love, Thou canst not fail,
Thy passion doth of right prevail,
And Thou art willing — I will rest
On the wide bounty of Thy breast.

I do believe at home, forgiven,
That both shall see Thy face in heaven;
Accepted in Thy love's abode,
And satiate with the peace of God.

" If Thou canst believe ; all things are possible to him that believeth."

I SIT before Him, and it draws to night,
But now with new-born hope I'll wait ;
For some have learn'd that yet He giveth sight,
Who heal'd the poor blind beggar desolate.
O Son of David, in Thy mercy great,
Hear me, that I may thank Thee for like grace ;
O Light, Light, Light,
Of old one blind, believed, and saw Thy face,
Light of the world, Lord Christ, compassionate.

I do not ask Thee for my poor dimm'd eyes,
Only, that they may see the sun ;
Give pardon, Christ, give, give in anywise,
The light within, the better day begun ;
Tell me Thou lov'st me, and I'll kiss the rod,
Then give, what Thou wilt give to me undone ;
O God, God, God,
Rise on my darken'd soul, in pity rise,
Helper and Healer, God, my holy one.

All things are possible to Thy great might;
    'Tis not new things that I would know,
Give the old faith to trust and crave aright,
    Lord, 'tis but eighteen hundred years ago
(One day with Thee) since Thou gav'st many sight;
    Pray with me, O my friends, that I may see;
        O Light, Light, Light,
Give me but faith, I look, I wait for Thee,
    Light of the world, Lord Christ, that healeth me.

As in an unknown tongue Thy speech I heard,
    Thy promise, " If thou canst believe ; "
But now my soul mounts up to meet the word,
    Now I restrain Thee not — I will receive,
Embrace, desire, expect the gift downtrod
    And doubted, — God, if now Thy will it be ;
        O God, God, God,
Thou knowest the light is sweet, I cry to Thee,
    Who gavest the light of life, give light to me.

EARLY QUESTIONS OF THE CHURCH.

"Master, where dwellest Thou?"

FROM many a plenish'd home
    They sweetly echo now,
The early quest, the early cry,
    "Master, where dwellest Thou?
Where, Master, art Thou found?
    For we would walk with Thee;"
Yet little heed the answer gains,
    Blest answer, "Come and see."

Where didst Thou dwell of old?
    Oft in a sordid shed;
The poor did have Thy household talk,
    And earn with Thee their bread;
But some that are Thy rich
    Oft seek Thee now, and fail;
They climb to meet Thee on the height,
    When Thou art in the vale.

We will subdue the proud,
　　The great, for His renown,
" We will go up," they cry, "for Him,"
　　But no, they shall go down.
Among the lost, the low
　　There shall He best be seen,
Who, when He touch'd the leper's hand,
　　Became with him unclean.

Master, Thy words are dark ;
　　Life yet her secret holds,
The mysteries of a mourning world
　　No voice from Thee unfolds ;
Thou openest doors in heaven,
　　But earth with tears is wet ;
Scant bread and bitter eat the poor,
　　The slave lies fetter'd yet.

He saith, " I am not dark
　　To them of base estate,
The simple, in his simpleness,
　　Reads all My strangeness straight."
He saith, " The slave despised,
　　His life makes plain in Me ;
All My hard sayings suit them well,
　　Whom I sink deep to free."

Leisure He giveth, and gold,
　Who may the bearer blame ;
But He had all, and did leave all,
　Emptied of all He came.
I know not — yet methinks
　'Twere sweet from all to wend
So once to walk with Him the way
　As a man walks with his friend.

He was despised ; — if I
　Have honour, woe's my heart,
I will Him seek and share the shame,
　I must to Him depart.
" Master, where dwellest Thou ?
　I fain would visit Thee ; "
Hark, hark ! Himself will be my guide,
　He answers, " Come and see."

EARLY QUESTIONS OF THE CHURCH.

"Is it I? and another said, Is it I?"

"ONE of those," He sigh'd at supper, "should
    betray Him;"
And they fear'd, albeit for love content to die;
And we love, but lips of men no more do say Him,
    Love's desponding words of wonder, "Is it I?"

"Is it I?" with Him they walk'd, their all forsaken,
    Yet against their own hearts turn'd distrusting
      sore;
Who are we, and what are we? that thought should
    waken
    Such a dread and such a doubt in us no more.

Still all confident, all calm in these our stations,
    Having known His word, we name Him, not afraid;
But from age to age He moves among the nations,
    And in souls of men is born — and is betray'd.

Ay, but not alone of aliens, nor the stranger,
    But the angels of the churches, while they pray,
And the saints who sing in peace, nor hear of danger,
    These have wrought, and these do love — and they
      betray.

By unkindness, for His sake, to brethren parted,
  By the casting out of sinners to their shame,
By the folding in of sinners fouler hearted,
  By all hard things done and said in His great
    name —

And for Him, by narrow thoughts of His blest
    passion,
  Evil envy, words untrue, and counsels cold ;
By their rising who should stoop in lowly fashion
  To the low, by lust of ease, by greed of gold.

O my Master, can it be ?   Do I betray Thee ?
  Wash me clean of this dark stain before I die.
Give an answer of deep peace to me, I pray Thee,
  To me mourning at the supper, " Is it I ? "

LISTENING TO THE WAITS.

"Behold we bring you good tidings."

DEEP the snow-drift covereth all,
  Stars do sparkle as they'd fall;
Hark! the waits come down the street,
Heart o' mine, their news is sweet.
Nay, I care not for the cold,
Hearkening thus good tidings old;
"Wake! you friends and neighbours, wake!
Thank the Lord for Christ, His sake.

" Count not our good news outworn;
Christ as on this night was born,
When to God the tidings came,
Clustering angels heard the same;
And He sent by Bethlehem town,
As it were an handful down,
Saying, 'Sing, for mortals' cheer,
Songs myself am used to hear.'

" Joyous on their mission went
God's good children innocent ;
Blessèd creatures, how they sang,
All the moonlit welkin rang,
' Peace, good-will — good-will and peace ;
This poor world shall find release ;'
Friends and neighbours, answer make,
Thank the Lord for Christ, His sake.

"What, and will you wake to sigh ?
We are old, we do but die ;
We must mourn, our children sleep
In the grave, and in the deep ;
We are poor, our toil is drear,
There is no room for us here ;
Peace, you wanting souls, e'en so
  Fared it with your Lord below.

" But once more He comes from God,
Master of this earthly sod ;
Then the proud shall meet rebuff,
Then the poor shall have enough ;
Then the mourners glad shall be,
Then th' oppressèd shall go free ;
Bide in hope, He comes again,
Sleep and rest, He comes to reign."

Hush, adown the snow-clad street
Faints away their music sweet;
Jesus Christ, this wintry night,
Stand me instead of warmth and light, —
Nay, I care not for the cold,
Waiting on glad tidings old ;
All my song shall henceforth be,
" Well is me," and " well is me."

" Behold, the Judge standeth at the door."

HOW dreadful is this place.
    As Thou wert far away,
  I slept in this my day,
Nor would Thy grace.
I wake and find that Thou art here,
And my soul melts in me for fear,
  Lord, of Thy face.

  Thou Judge of quick and dead,
    Now hast Thou found my soul ;
    O'er me Thy thunders roll,
  Me sore bestead.
O how shall I Thy glance abide,
No place is found where I may hide
  My guilty head.

  Lord Jesu, dread, yet dear,
    Thy faded eyes are sweet;
    Low at Thy piercèd feet
  I sink for fear.
O suffering Son of God most high,
If I must perish, let me lie
  And perish here.

Lord Christ, I have no plea,
  Thou knowest my guilt is great;
  Pity my lost estate,
My misery see.
Absolve, O Lord, my sinful soul;
None can forgive and make me whole,
  Jesu, but Thee.

" Till Christ be form'd in you."

I WAIT till Christ be form'd in me,
  My heart His mortal home would be,
The babe of God, and Him confess.
Drink of my cup, and reach me Thine,
Eat of my bread, in me enshrine
  Thy sorrows and Thy humbleness.

A very babe that crept the floor,
His stars shone through the open door;
  He gazing wist not what they were.
Partaker of our milk and meal,
When those His mother forth would deal,
  He sweetly watch'd her for His share.

With musing long my heart doth yearn,
The silence of His youth to learn,
  The striving that His soul would stir.
By faith, by searchings and by thought,
In eastern sheds with Him I've wrought,
  Many good days, a carpenter.

There is no glory, and no grace —
None, Thou Child-God. but in Thy face,
  None. Thou God-man, but in Thy mien,
For I do know Thee ; on the strand,
When as the nets were drawn to land,
  Thy humble follower I have been.

O Christ, and I did watch with Thee,
In the garden of Gethsemane ;
  Yet after I denied Thy name.
Yea, and amen — for now my tears,
God-man that saved me, all my years,
  Fall, for Thy worship, and my shame.

For me Thy precious blood was shed ;
For me they made that holy head
  Familiar with the burial myrrh :
My name was writ in heaven that day,
When Thou didst warm Thy sacred clay,
  And break the sealèd sepulchre.

Great Elder Brother, deeply dear,
Thy perfect love doth cast out fear :
  Thy goodness long my theme shall be.
I wait becalm'd, and draw my breath,
At home with pain. at one with death,
  In league with God because of Thee.

" Blessed are they that have not seen, and yet have believed."

L ORD CHRIST, the river is so cold :
    None see beyond the gates of gold ;
Our dead, once cross'd, have never told
    Ought they have found there ;
Consider us, that we shall go
Alone through that dark river's flow
Soon, to the land we cannot know,
    Though we are bound there.

We see but in life's narrow scope,
For Thee we search, to Thee we grope ;
Thou art Thyself our all of hope :
    O make hope brighter.
Make Thyself near, make Thyself dear,
Make Thyself strong to vanquish fear ;
Make Thyself most belovèd, here,
    So dark death lighter.

O make us satisfied, that we,
Since Thou hast cross'd, shall **surely be**

Partakers in Thy life and Thee:
　　Let fear have ending.
Albeit that sacred voice of Thine
We did not hear in Palestine,
Nor see Thy risen form divine
　　To God ascending,

We have one blessing more than they
Who met Thee on Thy rising day,
Who walk'd beside Thee in the way,
　　And Thee receivèd:
We know Thy thought to us did lean
When Thou didst say that blissful e'en,
"Blessèd are they that have not seen,
　　Yet have believèd."

" Christ also hath suffered for sins, the just for the un-
just, that He might bring us to God, being put to death in
the flesh, but quickened by the Spirit : by which also He
went and preached unto the spirits in prison ; which
sometime were disobedient."

AMONG the worlds of God lay one
    As if He had rent it from its sun,
And had been will'd to cast it far,
Thrown out where night and darkness are.
A world unblest, a prison dim,
It knew no visitings from Him,
But shook with sighs of them undone,
Whelm'd of the flood they would not shun,
And sent where th' unform'd billow rolls —
The sometime disobedient souls.

Hark, hark ! a cry of keen acclaim,
" What is Thy name ? — what is Thy name ? "
For lo ! into their midst come down
A spirit with a shadowy crown !
A marvel from the dead it stands,
All alien to those unblest lands ;
It speaks — unwonted morning breaks,
And the adamantine mountain quakes.

We know not more — but let that be ;
Is anything too hard for Thee?
Or wert Thou at the end of grace,
At that beginning, in that place ?

We trust to them Thy visit came,
For healing of their sins and shame ;
To us, who learn not all its scope,
An opening for a door of hope.

NOTES AND EXPLANATIONS.

NOTE 1.

"He is more present to all things He made, than anything unto itself can be." A thought expressed by more than one of the ancient fathers.

NOTE 2.

This hymn is an attempt to versify the following sentence : —
"How wonderful is the love which can discern the love of God revealed in and by deepest suffering, and which rejoices in the love in spite of the suffering. 'He took the cup, and took the bread'—symbols of a broken body and shed blood—and 'gave thanks.'"— *Journal of Norman Macleod.*

NOTE 3.

"My heart told me there is but one love." — *Lacordaire.*

NOTE 4.

It is noteworthy that Jacob does not get the better blessing till he has told his name, which is in fact to confess his fault. I am "a Supplanter." With the true blessing, which God (as his Father foreknew) had in store for him, but which he would not wait for, he receives a better name. Having confessed his fault, it is to be named no more.

It should be observed that in singing a hymn with a chorus, the hymn itself can be sung by one voice or many; but these one or many continue to sing with the chorus when it joins in.

Hymns with a burden are sung dividing the singers into two parties, and these never join.

A double hymn cannot be sung by less than four voices, the first commencing and the second answering.

Hymn, page 118, is intended for an adult baptism or reception into the Church.

University Press: John Wilson & Son, Cambridge.

www.ingramcontent.com/pod-product-compliance
Lightning Source LLC
Chambersburg PA
CBHW031058280326
41928CB00049B/970